W9-CPE-433

1. Electric fountain, Old Home Week [1907]

The Home-Coming "bee" which is so industriously buzzing throughout the United States, has stung Baltimore again—a second time within a year. Last September the City of Baltimore called her sons and daughters home to witness what had been done in rebuilding the city two years after the great fire of February, 1904; it also desired to impress upon them that with the burning of many of the old buildings many old-fogy ideas went with them.

There are many "first things" among Baltimore's best achievements. She produced the first railroad of the country, the Baltimore&Ohio; the first telegraph, and the first electric street-railway cars. While these facts are pleasant to look back upon, the real matter of importance is the fact that the city is now practically rebuilt and traces of the fire almost entirely obliterated, and new business ideas with renewed activity are infused among its citizens.

There are but a few references to "befo' the fiah." With new buildings, new streets, new sewers and the like, the municipality has little time for retrospection. The business men, on the other hand, are very much like Oliver Twist and are determinedly desirous of getting more. The city is preparing printed matter which will soon be distributed far and wide, showing the many reasons why its sisters and its cousins and its aunts should walk right in and look around before going back again.

THE BOOK OF THE ROYAL BLUE, September 1907

2. *Following pages:* Fulton Avenue [c. 1885]

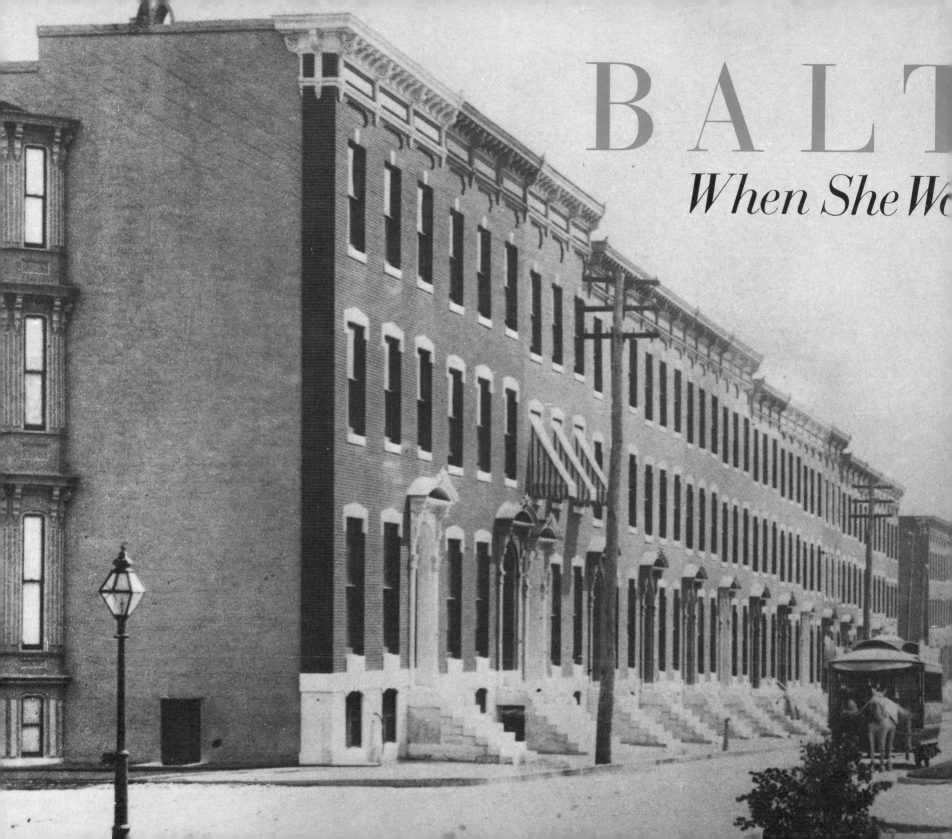

BALT

When She Wa

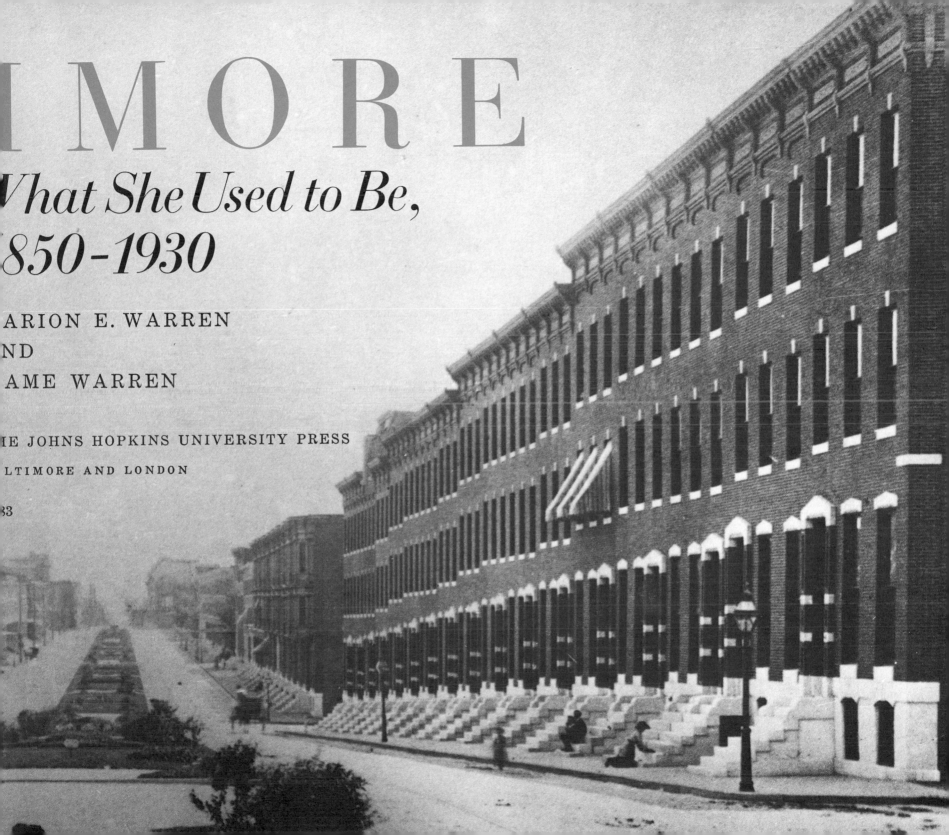

IMORE

What She Used to Be, 850-1930

ARION E. WARREN
ND
AME WARREN

IE JOHNS HOPKINS UNIVERSITY PRESS
LTIMORE AND LONDON

A ROBERT G. MERRICK EDITION

BY THE SAME AUTHORS

EVERYBODY WORKS BUT JOHN PAUL JONES:
A PORTRAIT OF THE U.S. NAVAL ACADEMY 1845-1915

THE TRAIN'S DONE BEEN AND GONE: AN ANNAPOLIS PORTRAIT 1859-1910

© 1983 by Marion E. Warren and Mame Warren
All rights reserved
Printed in the United States of America

The Johns Hopkins University Press, Baltimore, Maryland 21218
The Johns Hopkins Press Ltd., London

Library of Congress Cataloging in Publication Data
Warren, Marion E.
    Baltimore—when she was what she used to be, 1850–1930.

    1. Baltimore (Md.)—History. I. Warren, Mame, 1950–   . II. Title.
F189.B157W37   1983   975.2′6   83–48055
ISBN 0–8018–2994–1

With the exception of those photographs credited to The Maryland Historical Society and the University of Maryland Baltimore County, prints of the
photographs which appear in this book may be obtained from:

THE M. E. WARREN GALLERY OF PHOTOGRAPHY
48 Maryland Avenue
Post Office Box 1508
Annapolis, Maryland 21404

3. Front endsheet: Light Street wharves [c. 1890s]

4. Back endsheet: Pratt Street at Light [1916]

5. Photographic gallery of William H. Weaver,
147 West Baltimore Street [1873]

Acknowledgments

First, and most gratefully, we thank Mr. Robert G. Merrick, from whose generosity Baltimore has benefited for many years; fruit from the seeds he planted may be found all around the city. We hope that *When She Was What She Used to Be* is a pleasing addition to his garden.

We are indebted to Romaine Somerville of the Maryland Historical Society, to Mr. Sam Hopkins, and to Jerry Willse of Alex Brown and Sons for the roles they played as emissaries. Also, we appreciate the trust and cooperation given to us by the Department of Prints and Photographs of the Maryland Historical Society: Paula Velthuys and Laurie Baty were extraordinarily skillful in helping us wend our way through the department's wealth of material. The society's library staff, under the direction of William Keller, was most kind and efficient, particularly Francis P. O'Neill, whose mind is a veritable treasure-trove of Baltimore trivia.

It is our privilege to present here several impressive examples of the camera artistry of Henry Rinn, Jr., who published many of the classic postal cards of Baltimore scenes before 1910. We are grateful to Elouise Harding, custodian of the Rinn Collection, for her trust in permitting us to work with the original negatives made by Mr. Rinn.

Tom Beck of The Edward L. Bafford Photography Collection, The University of Maryland, Baltimore County, extended not only hospitality but also trust in making available to us the Hughes Company photographs in his care. Dr. Morgan Pritchett of the Enoch Pratt Free Library, an early enthusiast of this project, graciously welcomed us and our camera into the library's Maryland department. As always, the staff of the Library of Congress, principally Mary Ison and Leroy Bellamy, were generous with both time and knowledge. Michael Luby helped us to find a Baltimore gem at the Historical Society of Talbot County, as well as in his personal collection. The special consideration given to us at each of these institutions made available some of the best pictures in this volume.

Another favorite haunt, the Maryland Hall of Records, once again proved an excellent spring for both ideas and information. Phebe Jacobsen suggested a number of obscure picture sources, and Sue Collins provided microfilms of early editions of several Baltimore newspapers. We appreciate the opportunity to read those microfilms at the Washington and Lee University Library.

Sally Willse was an untiring organizer throughout this project. Much of the credit for the fluency of our text is due to the art of our editors, Mary Veronica Amoss and Jane Warth. For keeping our heads above water in troubled times we are especially grateful to Benjamin Vandegrift. W. Gregory Halpin, Maryland Port Administrator; Walter Sondheim, Chairman of the Board, and Barbara Bonnell, Director of Information of Charles Center–Inner Harbor Management, Inc.; Bob Mack; and Pam Jones were all instrumental in promoting this book in the Baltimore business community. We are indeed fortunate to have such good friends on our team.

The Johns Hopkins University Press has been most accommodating to us and our book. Their enthusiasm has been inspirational, and we are particularly grateful to Nancy Essig and Jack Goellner for their championing of our cause in time of need. For his artistic guidance we are, as always, honored to work with designer Gerard A. Valerio.

Many of the photographs on the following pages are from private collections, and thus have never been published in book form. For their willingness to share a multitude of exciting images we thank Beverly and Jack Wilgus, Ross Kelbaugh, Mr. and Mrs. Allan T. Hirsh, Jr., Gail Zlotowitz, Armand Shank, Jr., and Norman Vach. We also want to thank the many people who called us and wrote to us offering pictures that, for various reasons, did not fit into the format of this book.

We are grateful to the *Sunpapers* for permission to reprint several stories from both the newspaper and the *1905 Almanac*. The five essays that appear in *When She Was What She Used to Be* were selected from the dozens of articles about Baltimore that were published in national magazines between 1900 and 1930. In the interest of brevity and clarity, they have been edited, but their flavor and charm have, we hope, been preserved.

Sometimes even the most thorough search among historical records fails to reveal as much as our modern sensitivities might wish about certain classes, races, and ethnic groups. The portrait we present of Baltimoreans of years past is a full one, we believe, though in actual numbers some elements of society are illustrated more often than others. This circumstance probably reflects the fact that in photography's early years cameras were affordable to only a few, and that many vintage photographs have been lost.

Lastly, and lovingly, we acknowledge and appreciate the guidance and support we received at home from Mary G. Warren, Flora P. Chambers, Henry H. Harris, Jr., and Rodney Harris.

6. The approach to Mount Royal Station [c. 1899]

7. The Washington Monument [1906]

8. Lexington Market [after 1880]

9. After the great fire [1904]

10. Gwynn Oak Park [after 1890]

Chronicle

11. The Orioles [2 June 1911]

1661

David Jones, reputed to be the first settler in Baltimore, surveys 380 acres of land along the eastern bank of a stream, later called Jones Falls. He builds a house in the vicinity of what is today Front Street.

1781

Paving of city streets begins.

1784

A police force is formed.

20 July   Near the site of the Washington Monument, Edward Warren ascends in a balloon, the first such ascension in the United States.

1798

A society for promoting the abolition of slavery, and for the relief of free Negroes and of those unlawfully held in bondage, is formed in Baltimore.

1800

Alex Brown begins business—importing fine Irish linens.

1807

May   The Baltimore Water Company is established with capital of $250,000; cast-iron pipes carry water supplied from Jones Falls.

1813

William McDonald & Co. constructs the first steamboat in Baltimore, the *Chesapeake*.

1814

12–13 September   The engagement at North Point is fought by the brave defenders from Baltimore; Fort McHenry is bombarded.

21 September   "The Star-Spangled Banner" is printed in the *Baltimore American* and the *Daily Advertiser*.

1815

4 July   The cornerstone of the Washington Monument is laid. Construction completed 25 November 1824.

12 September   The cornerstone of the Battle Monument is laid. Construction completed 12 September 1822.

1816

The Peale Museum becomes the first building in the United States to be lighted with gas.

1824

General Lafayette visits Baltimore; stays at the Fountain Inn; a ball is given in his honor at the Holliday Street Theater.

1828

4 July   The foundation stone of the Baltimore and Ohio Railroad is laid by the Masonic Grand Lodge of Maryland, assisted by Charles

Carroll of Carrollton, signer of the Declaration of Independence.

1829

24 September   Baltimore's first public school opens.

1837

17 May   A new newspaper declares in its first editorial that "sensible of the intelligence and thirst for knowledge which pervades the population of Baltimore, a thirst which, beyond every other, 'grows with what it feeds on'— we have resolved upon the experiment of publishing a penny paper entitled 'the SUN.'"

1839

The Baltimore College of Dental Surgery, for many years the only such college in the world, is chartered.

1844

27 January   The Historical Society of Maryland is organized.

27 May   The first telegraphic communication, "What hath God wrought!" is received at Mount Clare depot from Washington, D.C. The message is sent over Baltimore and Ohio Railroad wires covered with rope yarn and tar.

1851

Jacob Fussell opens the first ice cream factory in the United States.

1858

18 May   The Alpha, the first steam fire engine owned by the Baltimore Fire Department, arrives in the city. Later in the year, after the Alpha had made a fine showing at a fire in a warehouse at the corner of Hanover and Lombard streets, the *Sun* commented that "the

12. Baltimore's first post office [before 1889]

work of yesterday showed conclusively that, with a few more steam engines properly managed, no fear of an extensive fire need be entertained."

1859

16 April   The cornerstone of the Peabody Institute is laid.

27 October   The first horse-drawn car goes into service on the City Passenger Railway on Broadway.

1860

19 October   Druid Hill Park opens.

1861

19 April   The first blood of the Civil War is shed when the Sixth Massachusetts and Seventh Pennsylvania regiments attempt to pass through Baltimore en route to Washington. Soldiers and civilians are killed and wounded.

1863

11 September   The publisher and editors of the *Baltimore Republican,* a daily evening newspaper, are arrested. The *Baltimore*

13. The Johns Hopkins Hospital [c. 1889–94]

Gazette reports that "General Schenck also ordered that these three prisoners should not be allowed to communicate with anyone for any purpose whatever, and that at half past eight o'clock last night they should be placed upon the train for Harper's Ferry, to be sent across the lines, not to return during the war, under the penalty of being treated as spies. They were not allowed to make any arrangements about business matters or clothing; in fact, the orders were the most peremptory and severe which have yet been issued here in relation to such prisoners. They were escorted to the depot last night by a heavy guard, with a view to prevent any communication between them and their friends. All of these gentlemen are married, and Mr. Joyce has quite a large family. It is stated that the cause of the arrest and suppression was the publication on Thursday afternoon of a piece of poetry entitled 'The Southern Cross.' "

21 November   The first Thanksgiving is celebrated in Baltimore, as in the rest of the Union, by order of the governor and President Lincoln.

14. Woodbury from Druid Hill Park

1868

28–29 January, 12 February   Charles Dickens lectures and reads from his novels in Baltimore.

24 July   The most disastrous flood on record occurs: a streetcar floats down Harrison Street; water reaches the second stories of buildings; most of the bridges across Jones Falls are swept away.

1869

There are fifty thousand houses within the city limits; value of real and personal property amounts to about $225,000,000.

1873

25 July   The most extensive fire to date destroys 113 buildings.

1876

5 September   The Johns Hopkins University opens.

1877

July   Railroad strikes and riots occur all over the United States.

On the 20th a riot takes place at the Sixth

15. Grain elevators, Locust Point [c. 1880]

16. Mansion House, Druid Hill Park [1867]

17. Location unknown

Regiment Armory in Baltimore. Eleven persons are killed and several wounded.

1880

10–15 October   The Sesquicentennial of the founding of the city is celebrated.

1885

August   The first electric street railway in the western hemisphere opens in Baltimore.

1886

5 January   The Enoch Pratt Free Library opens its doors to the public.

1889

8 May   The Johns Hopkins Hospital admits patients for the first time.

1893

16 August   Oriole Bill Hawke pitches the first modern no-hitter baseball game, defeating Washington, 5–0.

1898

24 March   New charter granted to the City of Baltimore by the General Assembly of Maryland.

1904

7–8 February   A great fire rages over 140 acres, destroying 86 blocks in the heart of the city. *The Book of the Royal Blue* describes the event: "The scene was grand and most appalling. The people who were attracted by the novelty in the afternoon were numbed and could not come to a sense of realization of the great disaster. There was absolutely no disorder of any kind. No panic, no ruffianism, no robberies reported." The fire could be seen one hundred miles away.

1905

Autumn   Baltimore welcomes the annual meeting of the National Women Suffrage Association. Featured speakers are Susan B. Anthony and Julia Ward Howe.

1909

The new building of the Walters Art Gallery opens.

1911

1 May   Women's Civic League sponsors the first Flower Mart at Mount Vernon Place.

1912

New high-pressure fire-fighting system goes into operation. In *American City* magazine, Mayor Mahool declares: "Without the big fire we would never have had this pipe line. With it, we would never have had the big fire."

1915

Regular telephone service between Baltimore and San Francisco is established; cost of a three-minute call: $19.00.

1916

Baltimore Symphony Orchestra gives its first performance.

1927

October   Charles A. Lindbergh visited Baltimore six months after he captured the attention of the world with his solo non-stop flight from New York to Paris in "The Spirit of St. Louis."

1929

Riverview Amusement Park, is torn down to make way for the Western Electric Company's Point Breeze Plant.

18. Jones Falls, looking east [c. 1851–59]

19. Jones Falls after a flood [1868]

20. Jones Falls, looking north from Lombard Street [October 1910]

BALTIMORE
When She Was What She Used to Be, 1850-1930

21. A daguerreotype of Pratt Street wharves and the city, as seen from Federal Hill [c. 1851–54]

Introduction

FREDERICK LEWIS in *Women's Home Companion*, July 1927

Baltimore is the only city in the world that puts crab meat in its vegetable soup. And it has other emotional claims to fame, among them, age. The first settlers came to the banks of the Patapsco in 1602; and a little more than a century later their descendants petitioned the Colonial government to authorize the "laying out in lots of sixty acres of land in and about where John Fleming now lives." Their petition was granted together with the further privilege of "erecting a town on a creek . . . on the land whereon Edward Fell keeps a store."

When the Revolution came the little settlement met the crisis with more men in proportion to its population than any other city in the Colonies. By sea it waged effective warfare against the common enemy, harrying its commerce, worrying its battle fleet and hauling many a rich prize into the placid waters of Northwest Branch. Because of its halfway position in the long thin little country, it served as a meeting place for Washington and his generals and in the winter of 1776 and 1777 it gave effective shelter to the Continental Congress. In short, Baltimore played an active and honorable part.

But it was in the War of 1812 that it achieved its greatest glory. The British admiralty became so annoyed at the privateering tactics of Baltimore sea captains that it finally ordered an attack upon the town. The British fleet steamed—or was it sailed?—up the bay; and the land force which had just sacked Washington marched northward, determined to break in pieces the heart of Maryland. The attack on Fort McHenry began on the morning of September 12, 1814, and lasted throughout the day and night but on the morning of the thirteenth, as all the world knows, our flag was "still there"—and our country had acquired a national anthem.

During the Civil War Baltimore's position as a Southern city in a Northern land was pitifully difficult. The first blood of the long conflict was shed in its streets; and the most decisive battle was fought within fifty miles of its gates.

It shouldn't be supposed, however, because of Baltimore's notable war record that it was concerned exclusively with sanguinary matters. In 1803 Napoleon's youngest brother, Jerome Bonaparte, sought refuge in America from British pursuers on the high seas; and at a reception in New York he met the young Baltimore girl whom he subsequently married. Their introduction was an unusual one, due to a button of his coat becoming entangled in the lace of her dress. Those Baltimoreans who knew the young lady best were inclined to question the accidental nature of the entanglement! But however that may have been, Bonaparte liked the idea of being "caught" well enough to come to Baltimore to pursue his courtship; and, just before his recall to Europe to join his imperial brother, he was married in great pomp to the merchant's daughter. The sequel was tragic. The young wife followed her husband to France but was not allowed to land. She went to England and bore him a child. In the meantime Napoleon annulled the marriage, placed his brother on the throne of Westphalia and forced him to marry a German princess. And although the validity of her marriage was subsequently attested by the Pope, Elizabeth Patterson never saw her prince again.

While the Bonaparte flurry was stirring society the town's soberer citizenry was busy with weightier affairs. "Baltimore clippers," the fastest ships that had ever been built, carried the trade and the fame of the American seaport to every part of the globe. They must have been wonderful little boats, those "skimmers of the sea" that were said to "start before the wind has time to reach their sails and never allow it to come up with them." They built up a wonderful trade and a wonderful prestige which were the foundations of the city's present greatness. Baltimore became a center of overseas and coastal trade; and in the latter obtained a leadership over its Northern rivals which it has never relinquished. Today it sends fully two hundred thousand more tons a year through the Panama Canal than New York does; and is likely, because of its position, to retain this primacy in ocean trade with our western coast and with South America as well.

Chesapeake Bay is less than nineteen hundred miles from the Panama Canal, whereas the Golden Gate is over three thousand; in fact Baltimore is nearly five hundred miles closer to Valparaiso on the west coast of South America than San Francisco is. The city's land situation is equally advantageous. It is the nearest port to the center of population in the United States and—a point that is fully as important in determining the magnitude of the city's trade—it is the nearest port to the great steel mills of western Pennsylvania and southern Ohio.

23. Looking west from Calvert and Baltimore streets on the **day of the great fire** [7 February 1904]

24. Looking west from Calvert and Baltimore streets [1906]

Among Baltimore's civic achievements it proudly lists the first railroad, the first telegraph, the first use of gas, the first silk ribbon mill, the first water company, the first Methodist church, the first medical society, the first college of dental surgery and the first lodge of Odd Fellows!

The intersection of Baltimore and Charles Streets is the business center of the town. Hereabout are the principal office buildings, department stores, banks and public buildings. The City Hall, a dignified substantial building of modified Renaissance type, harmonizes gracefully with its neighbor, the Federal Post Office; while the Court House and the Customs House are massive structures of classic design constructed throughout of white Maryland marble. There is a cleanliness and newness about this section of the city due in large measure to the great fire of 1904 which raged through downtown Baltimore destroying millions of dollars' worth of commercial activity on which the city's prosperity had been built. For the first time since the British stormed the guns of Fort McHenry, Baltimore faced a real disaster; and the way it faced it is the story of a modern city.

The fire was the greatest urban conflagration since the one which had wiped out Chicago in 1871. The horror of it roused the country. Offers of help crowded in from all sides. But the citizens of Baltimore made a decision in the very first days of their grief which had much to do with molding the latter-day spirit of the community. They refused all outside aid. Instead they formed a commission to rebuild the city on the firm foundation of its own resources. It wasn't easy. If it had been, there would have been no hardening of the community muscles, no waking of the community spirit, no strengthening of the community character. But it was done, this recreating of Baltimore, with widened streets and lowered grades, and improved docking facilities. And the bills were paid from Baltimore's own pocket.

Out of this ordeal came a new city of which we who sentimentalize about the old town know surprisingly little. The old Baltimore—the city of Charles I and the Calverts, of Jerome Bonaparte and his American bride, of Francis Scott Key and The Star-Spangled Banner—is a sentimental memory; but the new Baltimore with its coal piers and rolling mills and grain elevators is a stirring and not unpleasant reality.

Possibly it detracts a bit from the sentimental charm of the Maryland metropolis to know that every year it sells eight hundred million tin cans to packers in the state of New Jersey alone; that it produces enough straw hats to put one on the head

25. Lafayette Park

of every adult male in New York, Chicago, Philadelphia and Detroit; that it makes enough umbrellas to protect at least half of these hats; that it packs more tomatoes and makes more fertilizer than any other city in the United States; and that it leads the world in overalls, pajamas, middy blouses and bottle stoppers! But none of these facts detract from the modern Baltimorean's pride in his wonderful city, or his prosperity, or his general happiness. Nor do they detract from the city's real charm.

The fire which wiped out the unsightly business district left the finer parts of the town strictly alone. It was a most discriminating fire, eliminating the bad and saving the good. So Baltimore is that rare thing, an old city which is not dark nor grimy nor shabby, an old city in a new business suit!

It is easy to sentimentalize over Baltimore—not only for Baltimoreans, who can't help it, but for foreigners from New York and Detroit and Denver. Behind those red-brick fronts and up those white marble steps there is a mellow social existence and an intellectual life so rich in culture and appreciation that it takes the visitor back to the days of the salon and the patron. And there is—along with the gumbo Maryland and the Norfolk spots and the Appalachian bacon and the rock bass—a family and community solidarity worthy of the city's glorious past.

26. Fortifications on Federal Hill [1861–65]

THANKSGIVING DAY.—To-day has been set apart by the Governor of the State and the President of the United States as a day of thanksgiving, and will generally be observed by a suspension of business. Most, if not all, of the churches in the city will be opened for services appropriate to the occasion. The banks, the custom house and the municipal offices will be entirely closed, and the post-office will only be open during the same hours devoted to business on Sunday. The various markets throughout the city were open last night, and turkies and other fowls were in demand.

26 November 1863

EXCITEMENT IN THE CITY ON MONDAY NIGHT—Alarm, &c.—Great excitement was created in the city on Monday night in consequence of certain vague reports that the Confederate cavalry were approaching the town by the Hookstown road.—The alarm seems to have originated from the fact that several members of the 1st Delaware regiment, which had been attacked at Westminster, were pursued, as they stated, within seven miles of Baltimore. At half-past 8 o'clock a rocket was sent up from a point north of the city. This was soon followed by a report from a cannon. At 10 o'clock three pistol shots were fired four times in succession from the top of the Washington Monument, which has for some days past been used as a signal station, and one or two blue lights were sent off. At 11 o'clock all the alarm bells in the city were rung as a signal for the arming and meeting of the citizens. The members of the Union Leagues hurried with their muskets to Monument Square and Holliday street, and after being organized were marched, some to the barricades and others to the fortifications on the outskirts of the city. These bodies remained at their posts during the night, and at daybreak, no Confederates appearing, were marched back to their quarters. Most persons whose residences were outside of the barricades were unable to get to their homes after the alarm, and in some instances gentlemen who resided inside the line of barricades, and in close proximity to them, were compelled to march, under guard, to the guard house, and report themselves before they were permitted to go to their homes. The barricades on the north and northwest portions of the town were manned, and at some points artillery was placed in position, guarding the approaches. All the passenger cars of the city railroad were dispatched to the east end of the town, to be out of danger.

Yesterday the city was apparently quiet, no startling rumors being upon the street. Last night the barricades were manned as before by members of the Union Leagues, and there was very little excitement about the town. The running of the city cars was stopped at an early hour, and very few persons were to be seen on the streets, or at places of public resort.

1 July 1863

27. Crowd gathered at Orange Alley and North Street, to witness the arrest of a rebel, during the Civil War

28. Encampment at Locust Point [1861]

7

29. Barricade at Saratoga and Pine streets [29 June 1863]

The first blood of the Civil War was shed in Baltimore on 19 April 1861, when angry citizens attacked Union soldiers as they passed through the city on their way to Washington, D.C. There were no more battles: President Lincoln declared Maryland a neutral state. Construction of fortifications on Federal Hill began in August 1861, and the cannon there were aimed at the Maryland Club, which General Benjamin F. Butler believed to be a hotbed of Southern sympathizers.

Condition of the City—Military Preparations. The following is taken from the *Clipper* of yesterday morning:

"The excitement which has been agitating the public mind for the past few days culminated in one grand scene last night. Shortly after dusk hundreds of drays loaded with tobacco could be seen travelling through the streets. Surmises as to where they were going were indulged in by every person. At last it was ascertained that circumstances had led the military authorities to believe that the Rebels intended to attack our city, and would, in all probability, approach the city by the north and northwestern roads leading to the city. The roads referred to were, therefore, heavily barricaded with tobacco hogsheads, as many as 8,000 hogsheads being used.

"What made the matter more interesting was, that shortly after eight o'clock last night the 3d Pennsylvania battery from the Relay House, made its appearance on Baltimore street, near Calvert; the soldiers, however, were unable to state where their destination would be. During yesterday afternoon posters were placed about the city calling upon all of the members of the Union Leagues to assemble at night at their regular places of meeting, as business of the most vital character would command their attention. Up to a late hour last night Baltimore street was thronged with men eager to learn more concerning the proposed raid into the city."

In addition to the above, it is learned, on the authority of Marshal Vannostrand, that the avenues along the northern part of the city to Mount Clare depot, making in all sixty five streets, are to be barricaded. It is not intended to stop egress and ingress along the various streets, but to have the hogsheads so situated as to be placed in proper position to repel attack in the shortest possible time.

19 June 1863

THE DEFENCES OF THE CITY.—The barricades about the city are now about perfected. At several points, which were formerly blockaded, the obstructions have been removed and placed in more strategic positions. The work upon the fortifications about the city is still vigorously prosecuted, a large number of laborers, both white and black, being engaged thereon. Yesterday a demand was made for more laborers, and the police again impressed a considerable number of negroes for the labor. When this work first commenced, the darkies did not appear to relish the job; but as it progresses, they seem to enjoy it as fine sport. They are divided into squads, ranging in numbers from twenty five to forty. One is selected as the captain, who directs their marches from the station houses to the fortifications, and back again after the day's work is over. Each squad has its standard bearers, carrying the United States colors. They move generally at the double quick, and, having no instrumental music, they manage to enliven the march either by singing or whistling in concert. One squad came into the Southern station yesterday, singing "When this cruel war is over," and created considerable amusement. Upon arrival in town after work, they report at the station house, give three cheers for the flag and dismiss.

25 June 1863

30. Troops serving under General Benjamin F. Butler at Federal Hill [1865]

31. Baltimore Harbor [c. 1861]

ROMANTIC YOUNG WOMEN—*An Episode of the War.*—Though the realities of war are stern and bloody, they are often tinctured with an occasional bit of romance. There were brought before Marshal Van Nostrand yesterday four young women, from Winchester, under a military guard. Three of them were sisters, by the name of Green, who lived in the vicinity of the town, but owing to the various military changes were left without a home or protector, and were compelled to act in the capacity of camp followers. The other was a Miss Grey, probably a fictitious name, who, about twenty months ago, in New York city, joined the 5th New York cavalry, and participated in all the battles of the Peninsula, was at Antietam, and conducted herself like a heroine. She was regarded as one of the best scouts in the army, and her bravery was the theme of every tongue, frequently performing feats which the bravest of men shrunk from. Her sex was not discovered until the surgeon of the regiment found her incapacitated for duty, when she was sent with the others, above mentioned, to Baltimore. Miss Grey was raised about the Five Points in New York, and from her manner seems to have "seen the elephant" in its hugest form. Her hair is cropped short, and she appears as able to enjoy a fine flavored Havana, or roll a quid of Peyton Gravely's best with as much *nonchalance* as one of the sterner sex dare to assume. The Marshal, not knowing what disposal to make of them, and they refusing to go to Philadelphia, had them sent to the Almshouse. Miss Grey, upon being asked what she intended to do after getting out of the Almshouse, replied that she would immediately join the army. It is somewhat strange that she should have remained so long in the army without her sex being discovered. History records a ten years' Trojan war on account of the fair Helen, and the courageous conduct of Joan of Arc, but it remains for the present conflict to produce a personage who, if she achieved not the same notoriety, will at least for the present excite the curiosity.

13 January 1863

32. Light Street wharves [c. 1861–65]

NATIONAL CEMETERY DEDICATION

GETTYSBURG, PA., NOV. 19, 1863

The train which left Baltimore yesterday afternoon, at three o'clock, with the members of the City Council and invited guests, besides a large number of other visitors from the Monumental city and elsewhere, to participate in the dedication of the National Cemetery, arrived here shortly before eleven o'clock last night, having been compelled to move slowly in consequence of the extraordinary number of trains passing over the road, all adding their quota to the immense crowd which to day fills the streets of this now famous town. Although a great many persons had preceded us, it was not very difficult to find a hard bed and meals of pretty much the same character, and the opportunity was embraced quite eagerly by several of our party, notwithstanding we were abundantly supplied with edibles of a good quality (as well as liquid refreshment) by an excellent cater, Captain Thomas O. James. I must not fail to mention the fact that at Hanover Junction, on our way up, we were joined by a party of Governors, viz: Curtin, of Pennsylvania; Morton, of Indiana; Tod, of Ohio, and the Governor elect of the same State, Mr. Brough; General Cameron, late Secretary of War, Generals Stoneman, Doubleday, Stahl and other officers, who were severally invited by the members of the City Council to enter their special car and partake of their hospitalities. These guests were also regaled with several songs by the Baltimore Glee Club, Messrs. Homer, Root, Hayward, Ewalt and others, who, by their performance, greatly relieved the otherwise tedious journey.

The train bearing the President of the United States and his party arrived here before us, and the former took rooms at the residence of D. Wills, Esq., where Hon. Edward Everett, the orator of the day, was also quartered. Shortly after the President's arrival, he was serenaded by the band of the 5th New York artillery, when he made a brief speech, to the effect that it was important that a person occupying his position should not say any foolish things, and as he had nothing interesting to say, he might say something foolish if he should attempt to make a speech, and therefore he declined to say anything more than to return thanks for the compliment paid him by the serenade. As he retired he was lustily cheered by the crowd which had hung around the house since his arrival.

The band then serenaded Secretary Seward, at the residence of Mr. Harper, adjoining where the President stopped. He replied to the compliment, saying that he was now sixty years old, and had been, practically, forty years in public life, and that it was the first time that over any people so near the border of Maryland was found willing to listen to the expression of his sentiments in relation to national affairs. He was thankful for the change in public sentiment, and that the present war would end in the extinguishment of slavery, which he had always regarded as an evil, sapping at the vitals of the Union. He then retired, having made a somewhat more lengthy speech than the President. Both these officials were subsequently serenaded by the Baltimore Glee Club, and the President, who was visiting at the time at the house of Mr. Harper, came out and bowed his acknowledgments.

A great many persons, it appeared, kept the streets all night, as there was a constant arrival of trains, some of them at too late an hour to find quarter for the night.

To-day dawned with a murky sky and damp atmosphere, which was not dispelled by the appearance of the sun until near noon. At an early hour vehicles commenced arriving in town from all directions, crowded with men, women and children, as also were two or three immense railroad trains which came in early, and by the hour for forming the procession there were from fifteen to twenty thousand persons in town.

At nine o'clock the military portion of the procession began to assemble on Carlisle street, north of the public square, and the civic portion on York street.

From a tall flag staff in the centre of the square, and on all the public buildings and many private houses, the United States flag was displayed at half-mast, and soon the booming of minute guns commenced, and was continued until the procession reached the cemetery, and was formed round the stand which had been erected for the speaker.

At ten o'clock the procession moved to the cemetery by the route designated by Colonel Ward H. Lamon, the Marshal-in-Chief, in the following order: A detachment of the 5th New York cavalry as the advance guard; the Marine Band; General D. N. Couch and staff; a body of cavalry, composed of a portion of the 20th Pennsylvania regiment; a detachment of regulars from Carlisle barracks; officers of the Invalid Corps and others; two sections of the 5th regular artillery; General Schenck and staff; 5th New York artillery regiment; Lieutenant Colonel Murray; a band; Chief Marshal Lemon and aids, with the President, Secretaries Seward, Usher and Blair, all on horseback; Governors and other distinguished officials; Odd Fellows and Masons; Baltimore City Council; Baltimore Fire Department delegation; citizens of various States, &c.

Between 11 and 12 o'clock the procession was formed around the speaker's stand, the whole enclosed by a cordon of soldiers, and B. B. French, Esq., of Washington, one of the marshals, gave the signal for the ceremonies to commence. Rev. T. H. Stockton, Chaplain of the United States Senate, then arose and delivered a prayer, remarkable for its length. At its conclusion the band performed the air of "Old Hundred," after which Mr. French introduced Hon. Edward Everett, who stepped to the front of the platform and delivered the oration which has been given to the public. After the oration the Baltimore Glee Club sang a hymn, written for the occasion by B. B. French, Esq. The President then made the following remarks:

Four score and seven years ago our fathers brought forth upon this continent a new nation, conceived in liberty and dedicated to the proposition that all men are created equal. [Applause.] Now we are engaged in a great civil war, testing whether that nation, or any other nation so conceived and so dedicated, can long endure. We are met on a great battle field of that war; we are met to dedicate a portion of it as the final resting-place of those who here gave their lives that that nation might live. It is altogether fitting and proper that we should do this. But, in a larger sense, we cannot dedicate, we cannot consecrate, we cannot hallow this ground. The brave men, living and dead, who struggled here have consecrated it far above our poor power to add or to detract. [Applause.] The world will little note nor long remember what we may say here; but it can never forget what they did here. [Applause.]

It is for us, the living, rather to be dedicated here to the unfinished work that they have thus far so nobly carried on. [Applause.] It is rather for us here to be dedicated to the great task remaining before us; that from these honored dead we take increased devotion to that cause for which they here gave the last full measure of devotion; that we here highly resolve that these dead shall not have died in vain. [Applause.] That the nation shall, under God, have a new birth of freedom; and that Governments of the people, by the people and for the people, shall not perish from the earth. [Long continued applause.]

A salute of artillery concluded the exercises, the procession was dismissed, and the people dispersed —some to ramble over the battle-field, others to look about the town, and still others to their respective homes.

Among the marshals we noticed United States Marshal Bonifant, of Baltimore, who had the foreign Ministers in charge, and George Grover, of Grover's Theatre, Washington.

During the afternoon the 5th New York artillery marched to the headquarters of Governor Seymour, who presented them with a new flag and made a speech. General Schenck also made a few remarks.

The President and his party started for home about 7½ o'clock, and the Baltimore delegation at 8 o'clock P. M.

[The above was intended for publication yesterday, but failed to reach us in time.]

21 November 1863

33. Federal Hill from the harbor [1853]

36. Fortifications on Federal Hill, as seen from Light Street wharves [c. 1861-

34. Observatory on Federal Hill, demolished 1885

35. Armistead Monument and observatory on Federal Hill [c. 1887–1902]

37. From Federal Hill: domed building is the Merchant's Exchange (*see* 71, 72) [c. 1851–54]

38. From Federal Hill: dome *at left*, City Hall; *at center*, Merchant's Exchange [1876]

Fossils found on Federal Hill date from 8000 B.C. The hill, which offers an unsurpassed vista of the city, has long been a gathering place for Baltimoreans. It was there, for example, that the citizens held a patriotic demonstration to celebrate ratification of the U.S. Constitution.

In 1796, when David Porter formed the Maritime Society, an observatory was built on Federal Hill. From the observatory's tower (34), a system of flags notified merchants when cargo-carrying vessels were approaching.

In 1879, Federal Hill became a city park.

39. From Federal Hill, looking northeast

40. Baltimore Harbor from Federal Hill

41. *Following pages:* Gardner's Union Railroad Depot in Canton, Baltimore's first grain elevator [1873]

42. Camden Station [c. 1870]

Baltimore and railroads were forever linked in 1828 when the Baltimore and Ohio Railroad was founded and the first train service in the United States established. The railroad industry created thousands of jobs and was instrumental in making the city an important port. The Locust Point pier (45) was the landing point for thousands of European immigrants, many of whom settled in Baltimore.

THE COMPLETION OF CAMDEN STATION.—The architect of the Camden station building, Baltimore and Ohio railroad, has finished all the plans and specifications, and the work of completing the magnificent building, the erection of which has been so long in contemplation, will be commenced about the first of next month. It is scarcely necessary to refer to the causes of the delay in carrying out the intentions of the company in this respect, as one of the principal obstacles for some time in the way—the difficulty about closing Conway street—is well known. This, however, together with all minor obstacles, has been removed, and the building will now be finished in accordance with the original design, and, when completed, will be one of the handsomest of the kind in the country.

26 March 1863

43. Calvert Station, with tower, built 1855

44. Camden Station after it was mobbed and burned [20 July 1877]

45. Baltimore & Ohio Railroad Pier, Locust Point [1872]

On July 20, 1877, railroad riots were in progress, which caused the train dispatcher's office of the Baltimore & Ohio Railroad Company, corner of Lee and Howard Streets, to be set on fire, and the flames were communicated to the train shed. The rioters attempted to prevent the firemen from extinguishing the flames. The hoses were cut and the firemen attacked with stones, knives, clubs and pistols. But reinforced by a squad of police, the firemen stuck to their work. Other fires caused by the rioters were also started at the foot of Eutaw street, and on the following morning at the sash factory of W. W. Maughlin and Cate's lumber yard, from Jones Falls to President street. During the burning of Maughlin and Cate's premises, four cars loaded with oil were set on fire by a crowd of reckless boys, and the fire was quickly communicated to six others loaded with the same material.

CLARENCE H. FORREST
in *The Official History of the Fire Department
of the City of Baltimore*, 1898

46. [1873]

47. Charles Street, with Cardinal Gibbons' residence, *at left* [1904]

49. Monument Street

Charles Street is the axis of the town. From the Middle Branch of the Patapsco it runs north with only a small quirk at Barre Street and a westward turn in Guilford. It is, moreover, the dividing line, marking off the eastern and western sections of the town. Its history, growth and development are in a peculiar sense the history, growth and development of Baltimore. Once it was the fashionable residence street, but now it is given over almost entirely to business. Beyond Twenty-fifth Street, then known as Huntingdon Avenue, there was in the dim nineties only a country road. This road, very straggling, ran out into real country—a region of fields and streams, locust trees and violets. Charles Street from its rural atmosphere became Charles Street Avenue. This has an odd sound to barbarians, but not to real Baltimoreans. Then came modern improvements. The trees were hacked down, the streams piped, and the violets uprooted. But did the townspeople change the name? They did not; they simply added a more elegant word, and for some years the name of Charles Street Avenue Boulevard was common currency. This is slightly redundant, but it had the advantage of being very precise.

LETITIA STOCKETT
in *Baltimore: A Not Too Serious History*, 1928

48. Mount Vernon Place, looking north up Charles Street [1906]

50. Washington Monument and, *at right*, The Peabody Institute [1902]

52. Mount Vernon Place

51. Lydia and Nancy DeFord in Mount Vernon Place [c. 1900]

53. Thanksgiving Day [1895]

54. The Flower Mart [c. 1925]

55. *Opposite:* Revolutionary War Monument at Mount Royal Avenue [c. 1900]

56. The Monument to Confederate Soldiers and Sailors, 1400 block of Mount Royal Avenue, under construction

57–58. Unveiling of the Monument to Confederate Soldiers and Sailors [2 May 1903]

25

59–61. Battle Monument commemorating the Battle of North Point in 1814 [c. 1875]

On September 22, 1878, the interior of the Merchants' Shot Tower, southeast corner of Fayette and Front streets, an old landmark, and the most complete piece of work of that kind in the United States, was burned out entirely. In the darkness of the night the massive column of brick work resembled a gigantic torch, for its base was unscathed, while the flames flared out at the top, being visible many miles. While the members of No. 1 Hook and Ladder Company were assisting the members of No. 4 Engine Company with their hose up the steps leading into the tower, Mr. Simon V. Cullen, superintendent at the works, notified the firemen that there were fifteen tons of lead at the top. The men were ordered to run for their lives, and the last man just reached the pavement when this immense weight of lead was precipitated to the bottom of the tower. The absence of Mr. Cullen would probably have resulted in the killing of fifteen firemen.

CLARENCE H. FORREST
in *The Official History of the Fire Department of the City of Baltimore,* 1898

62. The Shot Tower—234 feet high, 40 feet in diameter at the base, tapering to 20 feet at the top—was built between 2 June and 25 November 1828, and used until 1892. Its walls, 5 feet thick at the base, are made of 1,100,000 wood-burned bricks, which were laid from the inside, without scaffolding. One million bags of shot were produced yearly by pouring molten lead through a sieve at the top of the tower; hardening as it fell, the lead formed pellets for ammunition.

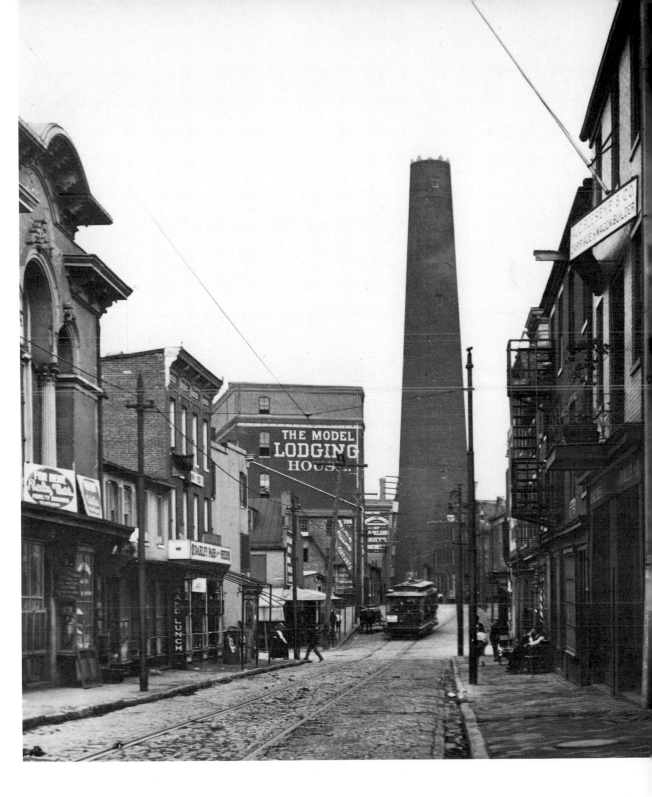

63. Corner of Eutaw Street and Druid Hill Avenue [1880]

64. Corner of Baltimore and Howard streets [1880]

65. Distinguished visitors to the Sesquicentennial [1880]

66. This obelisk, made of wood and covered with plaster bearing Egyptian hieroglyphics, stood at the intersection of Howard, Lombard, and Liberty streets [1880]

The Sesquicentennial of Baltimore's founding, which occurred in 1880, was the first of the city's celebrations to be thoroughly documented by the camera. The many photographs that survive suggest that neither effort nor expense was spared to mark the event.

29

67. The Carroll Mansion, East Lombard Street [c. 1900]

69. The original Maryland Institute, Marsh Market Space (*see* 235) [1868]

68. The Baltimore College of Dental Surgery, Hanover Street [1864]

70. The Women's Christian Temperance Union, 8 South Gay Street [after 1898]

71. The Merchant's Exchange (*see* 37, 38) [1880]

From its early days, Baltimore has been the setting for many notable structures, some of them remarkable for their architecture, but more of them notable for their famous occupants or for events that took place within their walls.

The Carroll Mansion (67), the last home of Charles Carroll of Carrollton, signer of the Declaration of Independence, was divided into apartments before becoming a vocational school. In recent years, however, it has been restored. It is now open to the public. The Baltimore College of Dental Surgery, the first such college in the world, opened 3 November 1840. The original Maryland Institute, built in 1851, was at that time the largest building in the United States devoted to the advancement of mechanical arts. It was destroyed in the great fire of 1904.

Abraham Lincoln lay in state under the rotunda of the Merchants' Exchange. Begun in 1815, the building took years to complete; it contained the post office, the customs house, a bank, a hotel, and the exchange reading room.

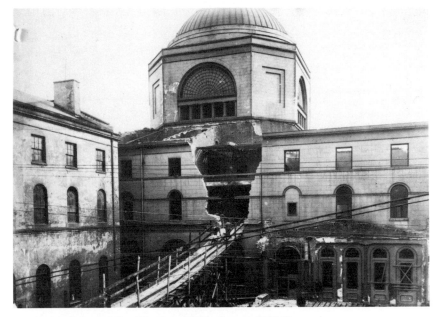

72. Demolition of the Merchant's Exchange [1901]

31

73. Laying the cornerstone for City Hall
[18 October 1867]

74. City Hall under construction [c. 1875]

75. City Hall was completed 18 October 1876

32

THE CENTENNIAL FOURTH

ANNIVERSARY OF THE NATION'S BIRTH

Adornments of Public and Private Buildings —The Shipping—Patriotic Emblems— General Illuminations

CENTENNIAL EVE IN BALTIMORE

The advent of the centennial anniversary of the signing of the Declaration of Independence has been welcomed throughout the entire country with extraordinary fervor and enthusiasm. In Baltimore for several days past all have seemed to be animated by this general patriotic feeling, and as if by a single impulse the national ensign, entwined with evergreen, flowers, portraits of Washington and others of Revolutionary fame, and many patriotic devices and legends were displayed from public, business and private dwelling places. Yesterday morning the principal decorations were described, but before last evening their number was considerably augmented, and there were but few houses in this city from which there was not some display in commemoration of this great epoch in the nation's history. The day was a legal holiday in this state by legislative enactment, but it was not fully observed. The markets were open until 11 o'clock, and more or less business was transacted generally throughout the city. Many persons left the city to spend the Fourth elsewhere, and all the trains during the day, in every direction, were crowded with passengers, some seeking the excitement of the great display at Philadelphia, while others were seeking the quiet of the country for a day of rational rest and pleasure. Five hundred guns were fired at Stowman's Hill in the afternoon by the democracy of South Baltimore, both in honor of Tilden and Hendricks and the national anniversary, thus combining their politics with patriotism. The harbor presented a beautiful appearance. The numerous vessels lying at their berths were decorated with numerous vari-colored flags, and were literally covered from stem to stern with bunting. The effort was grand in the extreme, and the water front of Baltimore never before bore a more gala day appearance. The ships of all nations vied with each other to do honor to the natal day of the nation in whose waters they were moored. During the day many persons visited the wharves and docks and viewed the spectacle, which was much enhanced by the fact that a fine breeze blowing unfurled to every advantage in the bright sunlight each gaily colored flag and signal. At night large crowds filled the principal streets and witnessed the illumination and the display of calcium lights, and though the weather was unfavorable for any great personal exertion, the people cheered loudly with every change of the color in the light displayed. The great centres of attraction seemed to be the vicinity of Baltimore and South streets, and the vicinity of the Concordia Opera House. For several hours there was a dense throng of people filling the streets and all was bustle and animation until about 11 P. M. when the streets bore their usual wonted quiet appearance. The stillness of the night, however, was broken at midnight, from the dome of the city hall, "Big Sam" rang forth a peal of welcome to "the glorious Fourth," while from every section came the ring of anniversary bells and the thunder of cannon and the rattling of small arms. The law against the firing of crackers and fireworks in the city was rigidly enforced, but from the suburbs the rockets red glare at frequent intervals lighted up the darkness of the night.

4 July 1876

76. City Hall and its changing environs [c. 1885]

77. City Hall [before 1903]

FAYETTE-STREET OBSTRUCTIONS.

Passers-by Near the Courthouse Put to Inconvenience.

The condition of Fayette street, between St. Paul and Calvert streets, is at the present time a consuming vexation to all who are obliged to use that thoroughfare.

The fence along the south side of the street is built so far out that it admits of only about three feet of planked walk, and between this and the car tracks there were unloaded this morning several truck loads of building rocks.

It is amusing to watch people who meet on this narrow boardwalk now that the rocks are there. It was bad enough when one or the other had to step out into the street, but to have to scramble over this long pile of sharp-pointed stones is a great deal worse.

The portions of the Courthouse fence remaining standing on Lexington, Calvert and Fayette streets will probably be removed within three weeks. The fence would have been taken down earlier but for a change in the plans for the sidewalk in front of the Courthouse. The sidewalk had been laid and finished, when it was decided to make it wider, and all of the work is being done over.

It has probable been 10 years since that part of Fayette street, between St. Paul and Calvert, was entirely without obstruction. This was due to the construction of the several buildings bordering on that thoroughfare. First came the Equitable, then the new Courthouse, and now the building which will adjoin the Equitable.

In addition ti this, the street railway company has on several occasions changed its plans for tracks—first single, then double, then single, then moving the single track to one side—each time involving the tearing up of the bed of the street.

As a citizen remarked this morning, it seems that since Fayette street has been widened it is narrower than ever.

18 November 1899

78. Court House, in Monument Square, under construction [c. 1899]

79. Court House [c. 1900]

LITERARY BALTIMORE AND ITS NEW LIBRARY.

A Princely Offer.

BALTIMORE, MD., Jan. 22, 1882. Enoch Pratt, one of the solid business men of this city, and president of the National Farmers' and Planters' Bank, has formally proposed to the mayor and city council to establish and endow "a free circulating library for the benefit of the whole city," at a cost of over one million dollars, provided the city will grant and create an annuity of $50,000 per annum forever, for the support and maintenance of the library and its branches. Mr. Pratt, in his letter to the mayor, says he has already, in pursuance of his plan, contracted for the erection of a fire-proof building on his Mulberry Street property, capable of holding 200,000 volumes, which will be completed in the summer of 1883, at a cost of $275,000. This he will deed to the city, and he will donate in money the additional sum of $833,000, on the condition mentioned. He proposes that a board of nine trustees be incorporated for the management of the "Pratt Free Library." No trustee to be appointed or removed on religious or political grounds. — *Associated Press Dispatch.*

28 January 1882

In 1857 George Peabody gave the city of Baltimore $1,400,000 for a library, art gallery, music academy, and the endowment of a lecture series. The building was finished in 1861, but its dedication was delayed by the Civil War and by awaiting the arrival of Mr. Peabody, who lived in London. The library became such a mecca for scholars that the site of the original campus of The Johns Hopkins University was selected because of its proximity to the Peabody.

For more than sixty years, William Walters and his son Henry collected sculpture, porcelain, tapestries, armor, precious stones and minerals, and almost one thousand paintings. In 1931 Henry Walters bequeathed the results of their efforts to the city, along with his home and gallery, and 25 percent of his estate for the maintenance of the collection.

80. Interior, the Peabody Library

81. Inside the Walters Art Gallery

82. Two views from the top of the 250-foot steeple of the First Presbyterian Church at Madison and
Park avenues, East by south, Mount Vernon Place [1873]

83. View to the east, southeast with City Hall under construction [1873]

84. The great fire of 25 July 1873: corner of Lexington Street and Park Avenue

On July 25, 1873, the greatest fire in the history of Baltimore broke out in a box of shavings adjoining the engine room of the planing mill and sash and blind factory of Jos. Thomas & Sons, on Park and Clay streets, in a thickly settled neighborhood near the center of the city. This conflagration burned from 10:15 A.M. to 4 P.M. before it was brought under control. During that time, four blocks were in large part consumed. The official report of Fire Inspector Holloway stated the loss as follows: 2 churches, 3 two-story and attic brick houses, 64 three-story brick houses, 18 four-story brick houses, 1 two-story frame house, 1 three-story frame house, 1 one-story brick house. The loss was estimated at $750,000, of which one-third was covered by insurance. The property burned covered nearly the entire area between Saratoga and Lexington streets, from Liberty street, on the east, to a line midway between Park avenue and Howard street, on the west.

A small volume would be required to tell all the details of this fire. Sparks ignited more than a half-dozen buildings several blocks distant in various directions. Roofs of many houses were manned by bucket brigades, which rendered effective service in extinguishing falling sparks. A number of persons were arrested for stealing property which had been carried from the burning buildings to the streets. The Sixth Regiment was assembled to mount guard, but it was decided not to be necessary to do so, after the fire was under control. Miss Craft, daughter of the keeper of a small store corner of Clay and Park streets, died from excitement and fright. John Cook, Jr. of No. 10 Engine Company, received a severe cut upon the head from a falling missile. Charles Nelson, substitute of No. 5 Engine Company, was overcome by heat.

The conflagration assumed such a formidable proportion that assistance was requested from Washington. The following telegram was sent: "To the Chief Engineer Washington City Fire Department. Send every spare engine and carriage here immediately. Henry Spilman, Chief Engineer." In one hour, engines 2 and 3, of the Washington Department, in charge of Chief Martin Cronin, were at Camden Station, having made the run from Washington, a distance of forty-two miles, in thirty-nine minutes. The Fire Commissioners of Baltimore tendered the Washington firemen a supper after the fire was thoroughly conquered, and the visitors left for home at 8:30 P.M.

CLARENCE H. FORREST
in *The Official History of the Fire Department of the City of Baltimore*, 1898

85. Smoke and flames [25 July 1873]

86. Looking east; note crowd in the street [25 July 1873]

THE VICINITY OF THE FIRE.

The streets in the vicinity of the fire were crowded with spectators. Ropes were stretched across the streets, at which policemen were stationed, and the crowds were kept back and prevented from interfering with the firemen. The furniture wagons, drays, and carts, did a thriving business removing furniture, and the charges were in many cases extortionate. Messrs. Brag & Son, wagon No. 2539, volunteered the use of their wagon free, and would take no recompense for removing furniture. On the south side of Lexington street the stores were closed from Liberty to Howard, and the pavements were piled up with furniture removed from the threatened houses. The people in the vicinity had their furniture all removed, and wagons were kept standing loaded up ready to move off at the approach of the fire. The ladies were much excited and alarmed, and the spectacle of ladies weeping over their broken penates might be discovered at every point, while some were running about wildly and distraught. A number of sick persons were removed from their dwellings, and in one case the dead body of a young man, who had died yesterday morning on Clay street, was removed to a place of safety, narrowly escaping incremation. The heat during the fire was excessive, and a number of the firemen became exhausted. Mr. Charles McCoy and other citizens carried around lemonade and other cooling beverages to the firemen while at work.

When the tower of Central Church took fire, the high wind threatened St. Paul's Rectory, and the furniture was removed. Brigadier General Carroll, James Chew, John P. Poe, and others, aided in removing the articles. A large number of citizens volunteered their services, and worked energetically to remove property, and many assisted the firemen. Conspicuous among the latter were members of the old Fire Department.

26 July 1873

87. Devastation caused by the great fire [1873]

88. A horse-drawn fire engine [c. 1870]

89. Fire and ice, 401–403 Exchange Place

90. Holliday Street Theatre [10 September 1873]

In 1856 volunteer fire fighters became employees of the city, and, slowly but surely, their equipment and communications were updated. It took the great fire of 1904 (*see* pages 122–37) to inspire a completely modern system.

91. Billows of smoke envelop a furniture store on Howard Street

On November 12, 1897, William Stahl was rescued in a thrilling manner from the fourth story window of the brick and iron building, Nos. 308 and 310 West Pratt Street. Young Stahl, who had been employed in the building but a short time, became confused at the cry of fire, and instead of making his escape by the fire escape in the rear, ran to the front window. The heat and smoke forced him to crawl out of the window on a narrow ledge or sill, where he was when No. 2 Truck arrived on the scene. The position of young Stahl was momentarily becoming more dangerous, and it required the exercise of good judgment and prompt action on the part of those attempting the rescue. Captain Heise saw at once the impossibility of raising the Hayes ladder on account of the network of wires in front of the building, so immediately ordered a thirty-five-foot ladder to be raised to the roof of the building adjoining on the west, the roof of which was about fifteen feet below where young Stahl was. The ladder was quickly placed in position and Captain Heise and his men ascended, carrying with them an 18-foot ladder, which they placed against the west wall of the burning building. This ladder was held in position while Ladderman Joseph Daley ascended thereon. The position of young Stahl was such that Ladderman Daley was forced to lean out some distance over the street and reach for the boy, who dropped on Daley's right arm. The rescue was attended with great personal risk to Ladderman Daley, who is deserving of the highest commendation.

CLARENCE H. FORREST
in *The Official History of the Fire Department
of the City of Baltimore*, 1898

92. Curious crowds watch a fire on North Howard Street, above Saratoga Street [c. 1890]

FROEHLICH'S
FROEHLICH'S
DEPARTMENT
STORES
MICHAEL HESS
JOHN B. FALCK
MICHAEL HESS
JOHN B. FALCK
HOSIERY, UNDERWEAR & YARNS
FROEHLICH'S
URNER'S
DIAMONDS
WATCHES
PIONEER JEWELRY CO.
JEWELRY CO.

Going to Market

LYNN R. MEEKINS, in *Collier's* Magazine, January 6, 1912

Of every dollar paid by the consumer for his products, the farmer receives forty-six cents. This is the statement of the Department of Agriculture of the United States. At one end, the farmer would like to get more than the forty-six cents, and at the other the consumer would prefer to pay less than the dollar. It is clear that the problem is to get rid of the middlemen and save that fifty-four cents. In Baltimore it seems that the simplest way to do this is to bring the two closer together in convenient market places.

A Maryland farmer may drive in from his farm, station his wagon in a great market, and sell his own things. He can build up a trade which gives him the profits and his customers the savings of direct dealing. In one big market alone six hundred wagons are accommodated with curb space, and this is only one of eleven markets located at points that will best serve the convenience of Baltimore's six hundred thousand people. And although the charges are almost insignificant, the total returns pay all expenses and give the city a handsome interest on the $1,263,389.03 which it has invested in market lots and buildings. So successful is the whole scheme that other cities are collecting details with the idea of establishing similar service.

Lexington Market is the most popular institution of the city, and it is said to be the largest market in the world. A great army of marketers—fifty thousand men, women, and children—storm it every market day, according to the careful estimate of the assistant market master in charge. Throughout the morning, street cars pour out their loads at the bottom of the hill on which the market is set. Half a block below its overflow has spilled down the hill and ranged on both sides of the street are piles of flowers, plants, and fruit, with busy sellers calling and with those touches of color that make a happy approach to the show. Up on the hill the market straddles the bisecting street, and all around are more open stalls. Every space is taken up, and the crowds wind in and out of mazes of benches, boxes, baskets, and people.

One of the first stands is a pleasant promise of the whole market. On a neat platform are bunches of mint, watercress, catnip, piles of chestnuts and chinquapins, and—what appeals particularly—rows of real country persimmons.

Inside the big sheds moves the mass of buyers, but these men and women are not mere buyers. It is more like a garden party. There is much pleasant greeting of friends, much stopping for a bit of gossip, much friendly talk with the dealers in the stalls. Women go from stall to stall choosing their purchases and declining to take anything that is not just right. Here is the elementary advantage of this sort of village market as compared with the new system of ordering over the telephone from the man around the corner: the buyer gets finer quality and greater quantity for less money.

In the crowd was the wife of one of the leading men of the city. She came to the market in her automobile, and when Lexington Market prices run a little too high she does not hesitate to go to the markets in the humbler sections of the city. She calculated that she saved about twenty per cent doing her own marketing, and as her husband is an epicure and as she does much entertaining, she secures a satisfaction in food which mere money cannot measure.

"Trouble?" She laughed when asked why she should go to all that trouble when she had servants to do it for her. "Why, it is one of the great delights of my week. I enjoy it more than a tea or reception. It does one good to be out among all these people in the fresh air, and you have no idea how many jolly friends I have among the market folks."

For the people in moderate circumstances, the open market is

93. Street merchants near Lexington Market [c. 1900–1910]

94. Lexington Market, northeast corner of Eutaw and Lexington streets
[after 1870]

the only means by which they can get the best food for the money they have to spend. As a rule, the prices in Lexington Market in the latter half of November are below the average of markets in other cities, and in some of the other markets in Baltimore they are below the Lexington Market's rates by from five to fifteen per cent. But the prices do not tell the whole story. It is getting the best material and getting it in full measure that makes the big difference in the final computation. And in this market there seems to be everything to eat that you can think of—all kinds of meat, twenty varieties of fish, poultry, game, terrapin, crab meat, oysters and clams fresh from the Chesapeake, shad twenty-hours from the Gulf—and every vegetable and fruit grown from the Lakes to the Tropics.

And the six hundred wagons crowding the curbs for three blocks and lining all the cross streets have each their own particular store of goods—the products of the farms and truck patches and gardens within hauling distance of the city. True, they do not contain a very considerable part of the whole total of food in the market, but they have enough to affect the prices and regulate the prices of those dealers who buy from cold storage and take advantage of demand and supply. Though these wagon men do not represent more than a small fraction of the farmers of the State, and are small farmers at that, in this village-market plan the little fellow gets a show, and if there is any profit in his goods it comes to him instead of going to the middleman.

"Some of those fellows who drive wagons could draw their checks for automobiles," said one who knew.

In many cases the wagon is a family affair. The husband, wife, son and daughter all come in with it and act as salespeople and each is equally keen to take advantage of any business opportunities of the day.

Market phrases fly about—the trade talk of the street market:

"We raise all our turkeys and do all our own killing."

"If you don't find it tender, you can bring it back. We've been here twenty years, and people know us."

"Mighty bad year for potatoes, but you will find this celery all right. Yes, we raise it ourselves."

"This sausage is right from the farm. City people think they can make sausage, but we country folks know a thing or two."

"Our chickens are fine this year. Some are incubated and some ain't."

"Best rabbits in market. Trapped yesterday. Plump and good. Only twenty-five each."

Voices filling the air, strong, fresh odors from the vegetables and flowers, and pickle stands and cheeses and the piles of candy and fresh cake—one thinks of it as an anachronism—a twentieth-century crowd in an eighteenth-century market.

Lexington Market is plumb up against the shopping district. It extends through three city blocks; its width is slightly more than half a city block. In each of the three blocks is an enormous shed: the first is 50 by 192 feet, the second 50 by 290 feet, the third 50 by 200 feet. Running down the center through all these sheds is a continuous aisle 20 feet wide, and facing it are the meat stalls. On each side are aisles 8 feet wide, and along these are the stalls for general provisions. Altogether, there are 1,200 booths or stalls in this market. On the streets and also along the cross streets are rough stands and curb space for the farmers' wagons. Owing to the fact that the streets are not wide, stable facilities are not provided for the horses. The farmers drive to their places, put their wagons against the curb, and then take their horses to private

95. Inside the Fish Market, at Baltimore Street and the Fallsway [c. 1930]

96. The Fish Market [between 1904 and 1908]

yards nearby. At other markets, where there is more room, the horses are taken from the vehicles, but must remain alongside of them the whole time the owners stand in the markets.

While Lexington is the famous and most visited market of the city, the others have their attractions, and some of them have larger sheds. Belair extends through four city blocks, Hanover has a shed 140 by 140 feet, and Centre is a series of three fine brick structures erected since the great fire of 1904, replacing cobblestones and slums, and housing a public institute. But—such is human nature—the new retail market is not popular.

Lexington, with its old sheds and its six hundred farmers' wagons, draws more people in a day than Centre sees in a month.

Here, then, is a contrast in the one city. Modern markets involving large public expenditures impressed the public as catering to the advantages of the middlemen, and so the people go more than ever to the old markets where the producers and the consumers get closer together. It is more than a sentiment, for the farmer receives more and the customer receives more; neither saves all the middleman's profit, but each gets a share of it.

97. Center Street Market [before 1910]

98. Lexington Market [c. 1900–1910]

Saturday Night at Lexington Market.

The Saturday market at Lexington market-house will afford to the curious a more perfect view of human nature in all its phases than any other locality in Baltimore. There are places where degradation prevails, but there is little else found in those localities, and there are the higher walks of life, but its habitues never meet the denizens of the localities first named, not even at a night market. But at Lexington market a lesson may be learned which will last a lifetime. With each succeeding hour the scene changes, so that those of the first and last hours never come into contact. On Saturday afternoon the market opens at 4 o'clock, and ordinarily it is quite well-supplied with all the luxuries and necessities of life. At the opening of the market, along Eutaw and Paca streets in its immediate vicinity may be seen family carriages, from which ladies have just alighted, followed by servants with baskets. Generally this class has the first chance and they go from one end of the market to the other, and inquire the prices before they begin to purchase, and then select such articles as they desire. Of course, at the opening of the market prices are higher than afterwards, and those who come first buy least, but they have the choice of the market.

After five o'clock a larger throng appears having come on foot, some with and some without servants, and they buy more freely. The first two hours of the market, however, have very little

interest. About half-past six o'clock the wives and daughters of the bone and sinew of the city, the mechanics, begin to reach the market, and while they do not pay such high prices as the first, they buy much more profusely, and chiefly substantial articles, though the luxuries are not passed by. These continue to come and go up to eight o'clock, and the curious watcher may see that they all, at least with few exceptions, procure that which is healthful and nourishing. About eight o'clock another class makes its appearance, to the annoyance of dealers as well as purchasers. They are young men and young women, who go at a rapid pace up one side and down the other, and frequently behaving in a manner that is exceedingly impolite. These young people average in age from ten to eighteen years, and go to the market without object, and they had as well learn at once that they are in the way of people who go there on business and for business, and would be much better at home under the parental eye.

At nine o'clock the poorer classes of people make their appearance. At that time the whole market is redolent with fumes of coal oil smoke from the lamps outside, and at this season of the year the market-house is hot and uncomfortable from the heat, generated by the hundreds of gas jets which have been burning for several hours. The best articles are all gone, and the meats and vegetables then left are of the coarser kinds, and the prices are reduced to correspond, and

meet the means of the purchasers. This is by far the largest class, and they throng the market until nearly 11 o'clock, and it is surprising often to see how little is left on the stalls after their wants are supplied. The market is then virtually over, but there is much left that is too good to throw away, and hardly worth carrying away to be kept for another market-day.

At eleven o'clock the market "Vultures" come from their hiding places, and they range in color from the blonde to the ebony. The lame, the halt and the blind, the very poor, and some too proud to confess their poverty, lest they should meet some whom they had known in better days, are all there, and the shins, necks, tails, bones and coarsest meats are sold at a few cents per pound, and frequently given away, while the dealers in vegetables permit their stale articles to be carried off on being asked for them. In this last class are many really worthy people, but their scanty garments attest their poverty. There are also those who are dissolute and reckless, and if they have not money, they have that propensity which furnishes them a bare subsistence. To the student of human nature, the Lexington market on Saturday night affords a school which comprises every phase, and it is really interesting to witness its gradations, even at the expense of snuffing a disagreeable quantity of coal oil smoke.

23 July 1873

99. Richmond Market, fronting Howard, Richmond, and Biddle streets, from the steeple of the First Presbyterian Church [1873]

100. Pratt Street

101. Unloading watermelons

Fruits and Vegetables.

Scarcely 6,000 boxes of peaches were received on Saturday, and the great piles of emptied crates remaining on the wharves indicate unmistakably that the season is drawing fast to its close. The varieties were principally Smocks, white Heath, Crockett's white and several of late yellows. Market men were buyers of the latter at $1 25 to $1 50. White Heaths sold all along from $1 to $2 75, latter for very choice; primes of other kinds brought $1 25 to $1 90 to canners, and inferiors, 70 to 80 cents. Only about 6,000 to 8,000 watermelons were on the market, which were dull at 4 to 8 cents—average 6 cents. The season will be virtually ended with this week. A shipping demand, mainly from the West, improved the demand and prices for sweet potatoes, which sold freely at from $2 50 up to $3. The receipts were 900 barrels. The supply of Irish potatoes continues very full, and prices are again easier at 60 to 75 cents per bushel, and $1 75 to $2 per barrel. There begin to be daily arrivals of cabbage from the West, which are green, of fine quality, and as a rule better than that grown in this state. They have been selling freely by the car-load at $7 to $8 per hundred. Apples are still very slow of sale at $1 to $1 25. Onions in light supply and demand also at $2 25 to $2 50. Pears—Eating, $1 to $1 50; cooking. 50 to 75 cents. Quinces, $1 50 per box for extras; inferior unsalable. The supply of grapes is still abundant, and they are dull at 3 to 4 cents per pound.

11 September 1876

102. Spear's Wharf and Federal Hill
[c. 1875–85]

103. Light Street, looking north [1906]

104. Shucking oysters

105. Cleaning oysters [1905]

Then, as now, the bounty of the Chesapeake Bay kept Baltimore's homes and restaurants well stocked with fresh seafood. The oyster industry, although seasonal, was one in which women could count on employment.

106. Oyster dredges [1905]

107. Unloading oyster luggers [1905]

108. *Following pages:* Light Street wharves [c. 1910]

109. Columbia Avenue and Paca Street [1911]

110. Unidentified

Among American cities above the half-million class, Baltimore is unquestionably the greatest harker back. Like the gentleman who was going to Bangor to get drunk, Baltimore is becoming a modern city, but, gosh, how she dreads it! With desperate tenacity she clings to every remaining fragment of antiquity. She still has lamplighters and alley saloons. Both diminish in number yearly, but Baltimore cherishes the few survivors. The last horse-car disappeared some years ago, but Baltimore still retains old-fashioned overhead trolley-wires, which make the streets appear as if festooned with cobwebs.

While the "bright, bitter cities down the West" are striving desperately to become spick-and-span and imitating the showiness, if not the magnificence of Fifth Avenue, Baltimore sets her face steadfastly in the other direction. To say that she is an ugly city is to give altogether a false impression, for ugliness ordinarily is construed as a negative quality, the absence of beauty. The astounding, the incredible, the downright fabulous ugliness of Baltimore, on the other hand, is distinctly a positive quality. The amazed newcomer to the city is almost persuaded that she has studied ugliness, practiced it long and toilsomely, made a philosophy of ugliness and raised it to a fine art, so that in the end it has become a work of genius more fascinating than spick-and-span tidiness could ever be.

GERALD W. JOHNSON
in *Century* Magazine, May 1928

111. Unidentified

112. Baltimore Street (*see* 69) [c. 1870]

113. Baltimore and Calvert streets; *left*, the offices of Alex Brown and Sons [c. 1905]

114. Baltimore Street [c. 1870]

THE KISSER WAS ABSENT.

Man Who Has Been Annoying Miss Maggie Wheeler.

A number of men lounged at the northeast corner of Baltimore and Calvert streets this morning, wearing an expectant air. They were waiting for the appearance of Miss Maggie Wheeler, 1244 McElderry street, who made complaint to the police yesterday evening that on several occasions a man had attempted to kiss her at that corner as she was passing on her way to her place of employment, an uptown bakery. They were disappointed. The kisser had heard of her complaint and failed to appear. Miss Wheeler's grandmother, Mrs. Sarah Abel, accompanied her to work. Several officers in ordinary dress were in wait for the kisser. On account of the publicity given the case the police do not think they will be able to apprehend him. Miss Wheeler had a particularly exciting experience with the man yesterday morning. The police have a perfect description of him.

16 November 1899

115. *Opposite:* Baltimore and Ohio Railroad Building, at the northwest corner of Baltimore and Calvert Streets [c. 1890]

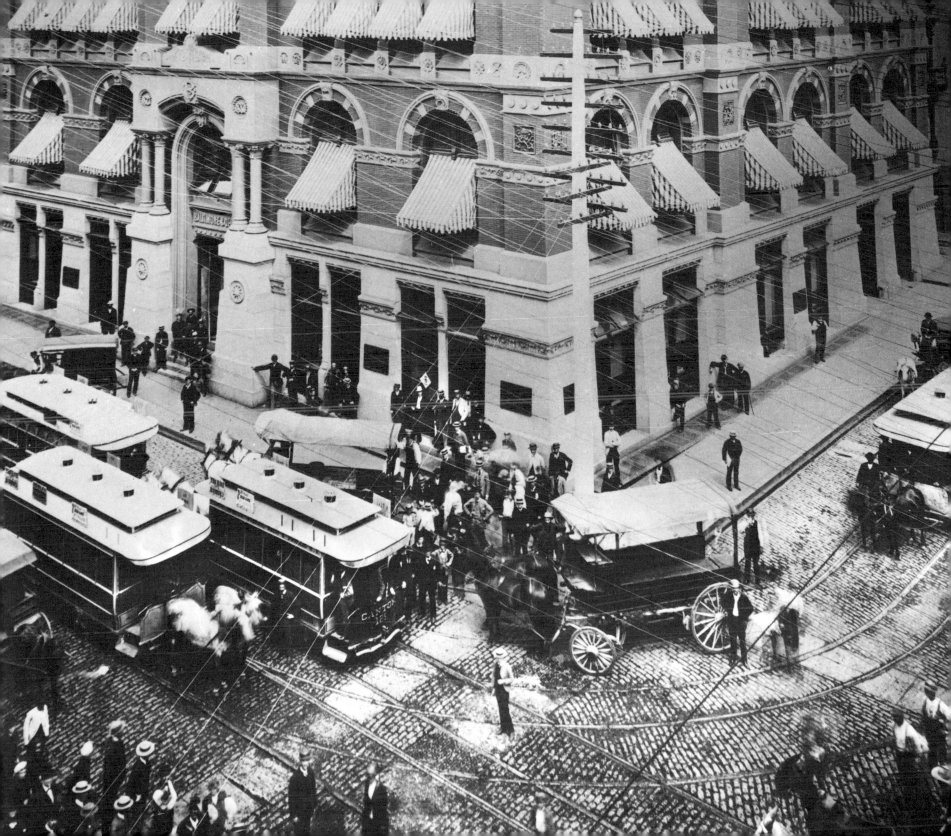

116. Altamont Hotel, Eutaw Place and Lanvale Street, accommodated 125 persons at a rate of $2.50 to $4.00, American plan [22 February 1887]

Baltimore's hotels were world-famous for their food as well as for their accommodations. Barnum's City Hotel, built in 1825, boasted a list of distinguished guests, including Andrew Jackson, John Quincy Adams, John Randolph, Daniel Webster, and Henry Clay, all of whom, no doubt, discussed the politics of the day during their visits. Jenny Lind, the famous singer, performed from the hotel's balcony in 1850. Washington Irving and Charles Dickens had drinks together at Barnum's in 1842. In his *American Notes,* Dickens reported: "The most comfortable of all the hotels of which I had the experience in the United States, and they were not a few, is Barnum's in Baltimore, where the English traveller will find curtains on his bed for the first and probably the last time in America; and where he will be likely to have enough water for washing himself, which is not at all a common case."

117. Barnum's City Hotel fronting Calvert, Saint Paul, and Fayette streets at Monument Square (*see* 61) [c. 1875]

118. Eutaw House, a hotel at the northwest corner of Baltimore and Eutaw streets [c. 1875]

WEARY WANDERERS

A Tremendous Crush at the Hotels—Thousands Unable to Procure Lodgings.

Conversations to the following effect were heard at every hotel in the city yesterday by *The American* representative, as he made his tour to see "the people in town:"

"Can you give me a room?"

"Very sorry, sir; we are full up."

"Not even a room on the top floor?"

"We have eight and ten in a room even there."

"Can you put a cot in the billiard room?"

"Billiard room? Why, every corner in the house is turned into sleeping apartments."

"Can't do anything for me?"

"Nothing, sir!"

"Good day."

"Good day."

Many a weary traveler paced the street last night, simply because he could find no place to lay his head without paying exorbitant prices. By noon yesterday rooms at any hotel were at a premium. "If the men would only leave their wives behind them," said a prominent but ungallant hotel proprietor, "why, we could crowd in five in one room, which we have to let go to a man and his wife. It's a crowd I don't like—that is, for hotel-keeping. The old lady will come along to see that her old man don't buck the tiger too much."

It was amusing to see the people arrive at a hotel. They would come leisurely up to the desk, with satchel and umbrella in hand, and, smiling, grasp at a pen to register. When the clerk told him that no room could be had, the face of the would-be guest would fall and he would gasp, "Not a room?" After going through the formula given above, he would pick up his satchel and silently wend his way to another hotel, only to be met with the same reception. After he had gone to four or five, he would get kind of used to the same old answers and strike out in a new groove. He would smilingly go up to the desk and say, "How do you do?" to the clerk; continuing, he would remark that he was glad once more to get back to the old house, and supposed his old room was ready and his fire lighted. But it would not succeed, and he would be turned forth again upon the crowded streets to wander about until some place could be found where he could at least lay down his satchel. Every train that came in at any of the depots was announced at the hotels by swarms of people pouring into the lobbies, and standing in line before the desk waiting to register. Those who had written for rooms weeks ahead were given them; but the majority had to look elsewhere. In some of the hotels the addresses of private boarding houses were given to the guests, and they went out to find rooms. At an early hour in the day some of the hotels began to turn people away; some found rooms at other caravansaries, and before long, they, like the Herdic coaches, hung out the sign, "Full." The crowds were far greater than at the Sesqui centennial last year, and the cry of the hotel people is, "What will it be to morrow?"

1881

119. Crowd on Cathedral Street watching for the parade [16 October 1911]

120. Cardinal Gibbons, *center* [1911]

121. Parade honoring Cardinal Gibbons [16 October 1911]

122. First Methodist Church on Light Street, south of Baltimore Street

INSTALLS 'PHONE IN CHURCH

Rev. L. M. Zimmerman Believes It Will Be Useful In Emergencies.

Rev. L. M. Zimmerman, pastor of Christ English Lutheran Church, has had a telephone installed in his church for the use of the congregation. In connection with this rather novel departure, Dr. Zimmerman said: "Persons often become ill in church, and a doctor can be called, the home folks notified and a cab ordered in a very few minutes. Again, often there is sudden sickness at home, and it is necessary to notify members of the family who have gone to church. All that will be needful in a case like this is to call up the church from the nearest telephone station. In case of fire, the Fire Department and police could be notified much quicker than without the telephone."

2 February 1904

123. First Baptist Church, Sharpe and Lombard streets [before 1878]

124. Musicians [1871]

125. The Holliday Street Theatre, built in 1874, contained 1,800 seats

Manager Kernan announces to his patrons and friends, the engagement of Albert Chevalier, the famous English Character Artist, at a salary of $2,000 per week, at the Maryland Theatre, the week commencing Monday, January 10th, 1910. (Next Week.) Mr. Kernan has assumed this financial risk in order to present in Baltimore the best there is in vaudeville. Not desiring to raise the prices of admission as is customary, when such great stars are appearing, he takes this means of calling your attention to this notable engagement and asking that you fill out and mail promptly the return postal, ordering your seat reservations.

127. The Maryland Theatre on Franklin Street [1906]

126. The Front Street Theatre [1864]

128. The Odeon Theatre, Frederick Street south [c. 1900]

OUR GREAT UNIVERSITY

THE LATE JOHNS HOPKINS' NOBLE GIFT

Brilliant Inaugural Ceremonies--Large and Distinguished Assemblages--President Gilman's Welcome.

THE ADDRESS OF PROFESSOR HUXLEY

The inaugural exercises of the Johns Hopkins University took place yesterday morning in the Academy of Music in the presence of one of the most distinguished audiences ever assembled in Baltimore. The house was crowded, every seat being taken before the exercises commenced. The lower or orchestra floor was reserved for invited guests, and was filled with representative men of the leading professions, while the galleries, which were thrown open to the public, were crowded to their fullest capacity with an audience remarkable for its culture and refinement. A few minutes after 11 o'clock, those to whom invitations had been extended to seats on the stage entered. Professor Thomas H. Huxley, of London, was escorted by President Gilman, and occupied a seat alongside of Governor Carroll.

129. The Johns Hopkins University Cottage and, *left*, the Rennert Hotel [1903]

13 September 1876

130. The Johns Hopkins University from the Washington Monument, looking west. Buildings fronted on Monument, Howard, and Eutaw streets [1903]

132. Johns Hopkins football team [1892]

133. Lacrosse game at Johns Hopkins [1906]

131. McCoy Hall [1903]

67

134. The Johns Hopkins University Hospital [1903]

The ceremonies connected with the formal opening of the Johns Hopkins Hospital yesterday accorded perfectly with the policy heretofore pursued by those to whom Mr. Hopkins entrusted the great purpose of his life. There was no unnecessary display, but a sincere and practical effort to make known to the public the aims of the institution and the grounds for believing that they will be successfully carried out. A careful perusal of the addresses delivered, which are published in another part of THE AMERICAN, will give to the reader, in a succinct and intelligible form, all that could be desired.

Baltimore will, of course, be the first and most immediate gainer, but the whole world will have reason in time to acknowledge gratefully the beneficence of the founder. As has already been stated in these columns, the most important results in the future will be the additions to accurate scientific information, and the consequent control of diseases and the lengthening of human life, but a feature which must commend itself as of the greatest interest is the school for nurses. Another avenue of usefulness is thus opened for earnest and worthy women, one in which they are not likely to meet with serious competition from the opposite sex, and where all their boundless wealth of sympathy, patience and gentleness can be brought into play.

There is no more genuine need to-day in this and other American cities than the presence of skilled and reliable nurses for the sick. Some of the schools have made modest efforts to supply this want, and have always found their capacity fall far short of the demand; nor have they always been fortunate in the parties endorsed. The Johns Hopkins Hospital can be relied upon to train and furnish nurses about whom there can be no cavil, the extraordinary facilities of the institution making imposture and incapacity almost impossible. The public must bear in mind, however, that the buildings were not erected in a day, and that great results can only be secured by patience and a continuance of the excellent management that has heretofore characterized the affairs of the hospital.

8 May 1889

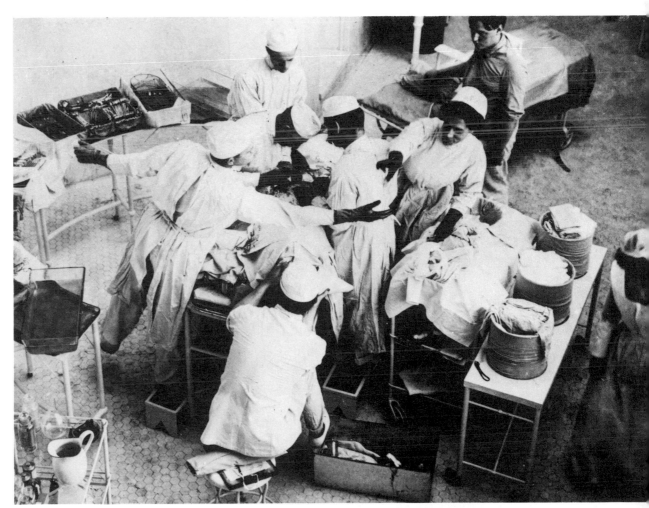

The Johns Hopkins Hospital, endowed by its benefactor with $3,500,000, was twelve years under construction.

135. Nurses at The Johns Hopkins University Hospital [1891]

136. An operation being performed at The Johns Hopkins University Hospital [1904]

137. A wintry day at Linden Avenue and McMechen Street [1887]

138. Pupils of the school at Howard and 24th streets [May 1898]

139. Fun and games in City Spring Square [c. 1912]

140. Saluting the flag at Reid Memorial Settlement House [c. 1915]

Behind the White Marble Steps

HARRISON RHODES in *Harper's* Magazine, February 1911

The new Baltimore risen from the ashes of 1904 is praiseworthy but not picturesque. The energy, however, and the progressiveness behind it are an essential part of the town's character. They had the first water-works here, the first lighting by gas, the first telegraph, and the first great railway. And it is just this blend of the enterprise so generally termed Northern with the easy Southern acceptance of the pleasant things in life which gives Baltimore its special note. These and another perfectly individual thing, the town's fashion of being a great port of the sea.

Baltimore is, if one may put it that way, the most inland of places at which you may take ship. Though through at least half the town there is the pervasive sense of salt water and sea-borne traffic, it is not of the Atlantic that one thinks. It is true that Baltimore's ships plough the waves of that and other, remoter, oceans. But Baltimore is the Chesapeake Bay's.

Concretely, it is the great bay and its shores which pile Baltimore's markets high with the best and cheapest food our country knows. The Chesapeake itself sends "fruit of the sea"—to borrow a pleasant Italian phrase—of every description, and from a very early spring to a late autumn the market-gardens and the orchards of Anne Arundel and St. Mary's, counties pleasantly named, pour fruits and the freshest vegetables from a real horn of plenty. You may eat Maryland peaches as early as June, and Maryland strawberries as late as October. And the air above is the chosen haunt of gamebirds actually eager to be roasted over the fires of Baltimore. The gastronomic centre of America. For the grateful city quite unreservedly avails itself of its advantages; it seems to be in a perpetual carnival of marketing.

It is not merely in Baltimore's clubs and in the houses of her aristocracy that good cheer is so abundant as to be famous. Every one knows the tales of feasting, and has heard the legends of high betting on races between favorite terrapin, devoted to sport during the half-hour before they enter the pot. Rare old wines, incomparable oysters, snowy crabflakes, ruddy canvasbacks—all these help to compose a picture of mellow tone. But what is even pleasanter to contemplate is the high-heaped larder of the humblest Baltimorean.

Of course it is not possible for the casual observer to be behind every kitchen stove and under every dinner table in so large a town; he must trust to his observations in the marketplace and to what chance acquaintances of the streets and shops can tell him. But he sees the humblest baskets go home to overflowing with things which are luxuries elsewhere. He knows that the moderately circumstanced can eat soft-shell crabs by the dozen, and the really impoverished buy oysters by the barrel. He will spend happy mornings lounging about the low, rambling, picturesque markets. Here at dawn country wagons still lumber in from the great highroads with "garden-truck," and in the late afternoon go home with tired but happy parties of marketers in rustic clothes and real sunbonnets. Here is a never-ending, cheerful confusion, and the satisfying sense that no one is going hungry.

Indeed, Baltimore, among great cities, would seem to be the paradise of the small income. Nothing is perhaps really cheap in this country nowadays, but by comparison life in the Maryland metropolis is actually within the reach of all. Supplies, to employ the term most comprehensively, are abundant. And house-rents are low.

The term house-rents is used advisedly. In all other towns of so great a population you must say flat-rents. But in all Baltimore there can scarcely be more than a dozen "apartment buildings"! This statement is meant literally, not as a picturesque exaggeration; though for a New-Yorker, for example, it is only by a far flight of the imagination that such a condition of things can be

142. North Broadway, looking south from North Avenue [1911]

143. Broadway [after 1889]

conceived. Baltimore is, broadly speaking, a city of small houses, the pleasantest large settlement of the moderately rich and the moderately poor in our whole country. There is plenty of money in Baltimore, but there are few great fortunes; the plutocrats do it there on a modest ten millions, and in something considerably less pretentious than a New York or a Chicago palace. The standard of expenditure is low. This helps the masses, too. And the curious land-tenure system which still survives from colonial days makes it possible for the man of modest means to own his own house. There are almost no freeholds in Baltimore; all houses are subject to ground rent. From certain points of view, this may be an iniquitous system; it nevertheless enables a family to settle itself at the beginning of its career.

On a modest working-man's income you may live in a delightful toy-like little red-brick house with fresh paint, green shutters, and the whitest of white steps. Your house may be only ten feet wide and a story and a half high, but it is a dignified, self-respecting habitation, and your castle as no flat can ever be. Near you, in whatever quarter of the town you may live, are probably pleasant squares planted with wide-branching trees, or streets gay with grass-plots, flower-beds, fountains, statues. Only in Baltimore do such boulevards run through regions of the tiniest, simplest houses. All this, if you are to view towns with some wish for the well-being and happiness of humanity, makes Baltimore a really comforting place.

There is still more matter for philosophizing. To the sentimental tourist it seems impossible to overestimate the artistic, ethical, and sociological effect of the white doorstep, which in both Philadelphia and Baltimore is the most prominent feature of the urban scene. Ideally, it is of marble; failing this, of fair planks of wood. There it stands, ready to be scrubbed each morning, to be painted each spring. It is the outward and visible sign of thrift, neatness, a kind of guarantee that within, too, there are cleanliness and all the domestic virtues. And happily for Baltimore, with the exception of a few sinister and ill-omened new streets in the outskirts, the white doorstep is universal. It adorns wealth. It mitigates poverty. It will be an evil day for Baltimore when she gives up this emblem of her civilization.

144. Unidentified [c. 1875]

145. Market Place [c. 1900]

146. 1028 to 1036 North Arlington Avenue, opposite the Pitcher Street branch of Enoch Pratt Free Library

147. *Following pages:* Workers at Theodore Ludwig's shop, 1212 Bank Street [c. 1890]

148. Old Defenders who participated in the battle for North Point in 1814 [1880]

The greatest resource of any community is its people: defenders, workers, leaders.

149. Ferdinand C. Latrobe, seven times mayor of Baltimore, and his old gray mare, Lizzie, in the campaign of 1887

The Old Defenders at Church.

The Association of Defenders of Baltimore in 1814 attended divine service yesterday morning. This year the members to the number of seventeen assembled at the city hall at 10.30 o'clock and proceeded to High-street M. E. church, where the annual sermon was preached by Rev. W. H. Chapman, pastor, from First Timothy 1, 18: "That thou mightest war a good warfare." The history of the world, the preacher said, was largely a history of war. It had marked every age and every century. Most of the nations that now exist were largely indebted for their greatness and strength to the mighty struggles through which they had passed, and which in some instances was waged with wonderful persistency and stubbornness. He referred to several of the most prominent wars and dwelt at some length upon the war for independence, which he regarded as more than justifiable. The war of 1812–14 was equally a just one. The events of that war, particularly those occurring in the vicinity of Washington and Baltimore, were minutely described by the preacher, who paid a touching tribute to his aged hearers who participated in the movements culminating in the final repulse of the British. The scholars of the Sunday school were seated in the gallery, and as the veterans entered the edifice welcomed them by singing the hymn, "Stand on the Rock." The names and ages of the members of the association present are as follows: Major Joshua Dryden, president, 84 years; Asbury Jarrett, treasurer, 81 years; Colonel Nicholas Brewer, secretary, 87 years; John Ijams, marshal, 87 years; Wm. Batchelor, ensign, 80 years; Samuel Jennings, ensign, 79 years; John J. Daneker, 78 years; Geo. Boss, 82 years; Wm. Stites, 80 years; Richard G. Cox, 79 years; Wm. Keener, 82 years; Nathaniel Watts, 81 years; Jesse Armiger, 76 years; Jacob Beam, 84 years; Henry Lightner, 79 years; David Whitson, 86 years, and Dr. Montgomery, 79 years. Mr. Keener, on invitation of Dr. Montgomery, rode in his carriage from the city hall to the church.

11 September 1876

150. Officers of the North Eastern Police Station

151. Employees of Dorman and Smyth Hardware warehouse [c. 1930]

152. Milk wagons of the Western Maryland Dairy on a street in Baltimore [c. 1910]

EMPIRE STEAM LAUNDRY,
Cor. Fayette and Front Streets,

A. J. MABBETT, Proprietor.   **BALTIMORE, MD.**

Our Steam Power Collar and Cuff Ironing Machine,
THE ONLY ONE IN THE STATE,
100 COLLARS IRONED EVERY 5 MINUTES!

CAPACITY: Twelve Hundred Dozen Collars per Day.

The ONLY Laundry in the CITY or STATE that can Launder your Collars and Cuffs EQUAL to NEW.

SATISFACTION GUARANTEED.

J. F. HUGHES, PHOTOGRAPHER, BALTIMORE.

153. Mail "truck" [c. 1912]

154. The Empire Steam Laundry, Fayette and Front streets [c. 1886]

WHIRLING WHEELMEN.

Interesting Exhibition by Bicyclists at Druid Hill Park.

The bicycle tournament was postponed yesterday until some future and more auspicious day. The primary cause of the postponement was the weather. The little spatter of rain about noon gave promise of a settled drizzle, and this kept the visiting wheelmen away. In Philadelphia it was raining hard, and no doubt those who intended coming over from there thought that the same rain was falling here. It did not, however, for after 2 o'clock it cleared off and the sun shone through the clouds. A large crowd collected around the shores of the Druid Lake, anxious to see the sport, and rather than they should be disappointed, it was arranged by the managers of the meet that one or two races should be run by the bicyclers who were there. There were one or two of the Washington Club on hand, and nearly all of the Baltimore Bicycle Club men were out in uniform, with their machines. It was arranged that three scrub races should be run for prizes to be given hereafter. F. C. South was appointed judge, with T. J. Shryock, referee and manager; Prof. Jno. McGraw, starter; J. H. Cottman timer. The track was around the great lake, the finish being on the side next the Madison avenue gate. The crowd that pressed along the track was very annoying, and on two occasions wheelmen who were speeding up and down came in contact with the small boy, and "horse and rider blent" immediately with the unfortunate urchin in the sand.

In the first race, which was for a half mile, Messrs. H. H. Duker, F. Fisher, John B. Morris and Samuel Clark, started. Morris got a bad start, and owing to the fact that he was riding a machine that he was not familiar with, was unable to make up the gap. The race was a swift one. Duker leaned over on his handles and worked the lead through to the finish in 1 minute 40 seconds, Fisher second, Clark third, Morris fourth. All four, however, finished only about four yards apart.

The second race was a two mile contest, for all comers. The starters were H. Owen and Samuel Barber, Capitol Bi. C.; Wiesenfeld and Dr. Wilcox, of Baltimore. Mr. Owen, the tall gentleman with the 60 inch machine—the same who won the race at Newington on Tuesday, scooped this also easily. In fact, he played with the others and won as he liked, in 7 minutes 52 seconds, Barber second, Wiesenfeld third, Wilcox fourth.

The third race was a mile and a-half. Starters, H. H. Duker, F. Fisher, E. Bennett and E. Le Cato. This was won also by Duker in 6 minutes 9¾ seconds, the others being close behind.

It has not as yet been decided when the regular meet will come off, but it will be in a short time.

c. 1882

156. 1831 West Lafayette Avenue [c. 1910]

155. N. Tip Slee sold bicycles at 2310–2312 Madison Avenue from 1895 to 1901. By 1903 he was marketing gasoline engines

157. Grocery store, 2785 North Avenue

Dr. BRANDRETH'S OFFICES, for the sale of the VEGETABLE UNIVERSAL PILLS, wholesale and retail, are at No. 80 SOUTH CHARLES street, 3d door from Pratt street, directly opposite the Ohio and Baltimore Rail Road Depot, and 72 SARATOGA street, between Howard and Eutaw sts.

These Pills have now attained an unprecedented popularity; so great indeed that a number of Druggists are constantly engaged in imitating them. This circumstance should induce those who recommend their friends to use the Brandreth Pills, at the same time to be careful to impress upon their minds the necessity of avoiding Druggists, as it is in their stores the counterfeits are usually found.

Let all invalids bear in mind, that the human frame is subject to only one disease, an impurity of the blood, which, by impeding its circulation, brings about a derangement of the system, and unless soon removed, ultimately settles upon some particular part of the body, causing pains, swellings, ulcerations, &c. &c. and that this impurity can be effectu-ally removed from the body by continually purging it with the Brandreth Pills, is fully proved by the cures they have effected.

Fever and ague, dropsy, inflammations, dyspepsia, nervous affections, and all diseases of the liver, gout, rheumatism, lumbago, epilepsy, apoplexy, paralysis, palsy, measles, whooping cough, scrofula, king's evil, and all cutaneous diseases, fits, mental derangement, etc. in short, every disease incident to the human frame, as there never has yet been an in-stance of these Pills not giving relief, except where nature has been entirely exhausted, Provided this is not the case, however old and obstinate it may be, perseverance and a strict adherence to the directions, will be certain to ensure a cure. The increasing sale in all parts of the United States, fully demon-strate the virtue and efficacy of the Brandreth Pills.

No danger can possibly arise from the use of them. —The testimony of thousands of persons who have been cured with the medicine, satisfactorily prove this.

Remember, no Drug Store has the genuine Bran-dreth Pills for sale.   m17-6m

17 May 1837

158. J. B. Bayley's Drug Store, Madison Avenue and McMechen Street

159. Hutzler Brothers, founded in 1858, kept expanding on its original Howard Street site until 1887, when these structures were demolished to make way for the Palace Building

160. 267 West Baltimore Street, between Eutaw and Howard streets [1880]

161. Southeast corner of Eutaw and Lexington streets [c. 1873–1885]

162. 21 East Lombard Street [1902–3]

163. 401 Exchange Place [c. 1896]

164. Office workers at Gardiner Dairy [c. 1910]

165. The piano factory of Charles M. Stieff

SPANISH SEGAR AND TOBACCO WAREHOUSE, No. 8 North Howard street, Baltimore.—IMPORTANT NOTICE.—The subscribers respectfully inform Southern and Western Merchants that they have a large and well selected stock of Tobacco and Segars on hand, selected expressly for those markets, and warranted to be of superior quality, which will be disposed of on reasonable terms, and the inducement such as cannot fail to give satisfaction.
In Store—
213 boxes E. Brown's ne plus ultra No. 1 Tobacco
  107 do   Bridge's & Allen's Honey dew do.
  111 do   (Jesse Hare's) Dulcissimis
   70 do   (T. Carmo)   do   do.
  128 do   small lumps, 5's, 8's, and 12 to lb.
   14 do   do   32's to lb.
   70 do   low priced to lumps
  113 do   5's rolls Tobacco
   18 do   Ladies Twist do
   50 gross Snuff Bottles.
70,000 Havana Segars, various brands
45,000 Trabucos (entitled to debenture)
140,000 Domestic manufacture Spanish do.
600,000 half and ¾ Spanish   do.
  With every description of Snuff put up neatly to order by   JOHN HACK & CO. m17-1m

17 May 1837

SCARCITY OF ICE.—One of the greatest luxuries during the continuance of this hot weather is a beautiful supply of ice. Within the past few days, however, the ice dealers have not been able to supply half the demand, and yesterday the article was not to be had hardly at any price. It is stated that the Government had appropriated a considerable quantity loaded for dealers, for hospital purposes, which produced the scarcity. The wants of the community will be fully met in a day or two, as several vessels loaded with ice arrived here last night, and more are on the way.

12 August 1863

166. Cochran-Oler Ice Company employed 500 people: 250 delivery teams covered the entire city daily between 1885 and 1898

167. Bethlehem Steel Plant, Sparrow's Point, where operations began in 1889

168. The building of First Presbyterian Church, corner of Madison and Park avenues. It was from this steeple that William H. Weaver took his panoramic views of Baltimore (*see* 82, 83, 99) [1873]

169. Rowhouses being built on Randall and Belt Streets

170. Progress photograph, 17 October 1904, of Maryland Casualty Building, opposite City Hall

171. Looking north on Calvert Street from the Equitable Trust Building. Court House is under construction in foreground [1900]

172. *Following pages:* The Carroll Park Shops of United Railways & Electric Company [1901]

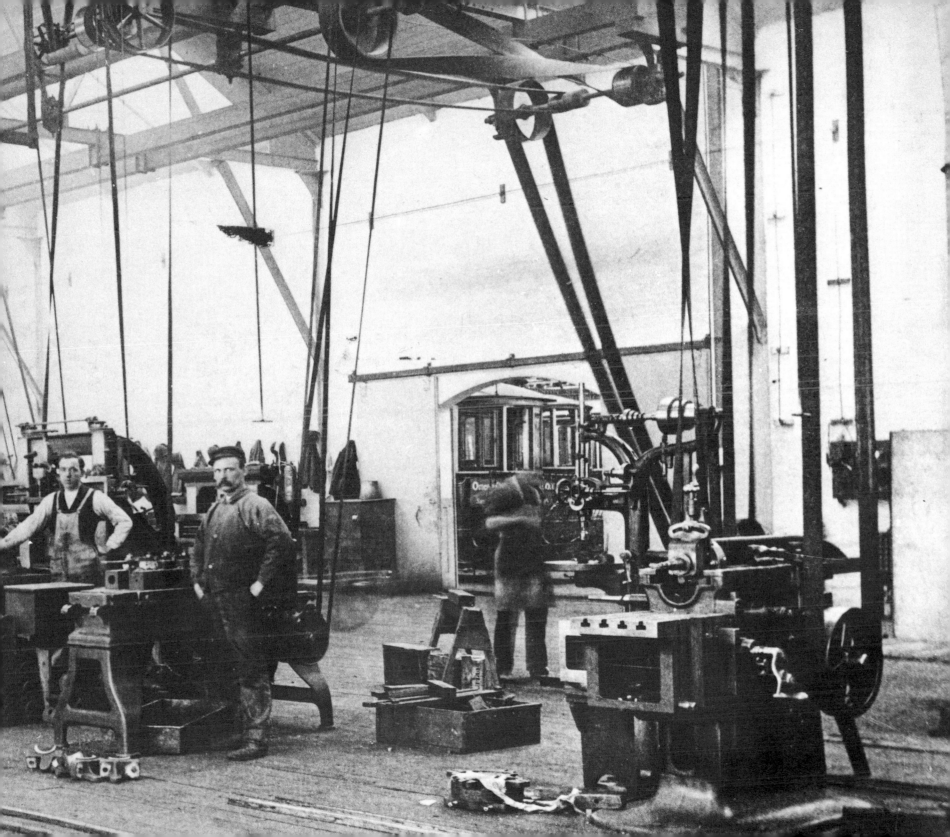

173. Horse-drawn streetcars began operating in Baltimore in 1859, on iron rails in a circuitous route from the foot of Broadway to Baltimore and South streets

Streetcars were a pervasive element of city life in Baltimore for more than a century. Among the most unusual was a small-scale "dummy" locomotive and string of cars that meandered through Druid Hill Park. The name describes the engine (*see* 207), which resembled a coach. Apparently the sight of a locomotive frightened horses, but a passenger car did not. The system ran from 1865 to 1877.

RAILWAY MOTOR FOR BALTIMORE.

The Cars of the Citizens' Line to be Propelled by Steam.

Several days ago the announcement was made in the GAZETTE of the intention of the Citizens' passenger railway line to introduce steam as a motor on their cars. The president of the company, Mr. James S. Hagerty, has given the subject a very careful and thorough consideration and has just had built by Baldwin & Co., of Philadelphia, a model engine, called the "F. C. Latrobe," in honor of the mayor of Baltimore, which will arrive at President-street depot early this morning. A public test will take place to-morrow or Friday, the precise time and place for holding which will be announced through the public press and the public invited to witness its operation. In an interview with Mr. Hagerty yesterday he expressed his entire confidence in the perfect success of the motor, which he has had constructed after his own ideas, and is assured there will be no difficulty in its readily drawing one or more cars up the heaviest grades on the line of the Citizens' railway. Unlike the motors in operation in Philadelphia and other cities, the "Latrobe" is separate and distinct from the car, occupying about the same space in front as the horses and the regular width of the track. By this means the heat caused when the boiler is placed in the forward part of the car is done away with. Its operations are noiseless, and the smoke is consumed, thus removing two serious objections to the use of steam on street railways. One man is all that is necessary to direct the movements of the motor, which are very simple, and the applications for starting and stopping are such as to prevent jarring in the former and accidents in the latter instance. Any desired rate of speed can be attained, and in other respects the invention is said to be perfect. The cost of each motor is about $3,000, and in the event of the experiment proving successful—of which there seems to be little, if any, doubt—Mr. Hagerty announces his intention of dispensing altogether with the use of horses on his line, and to substitute in their place the new steam motors. Thirty of them, he says, can be built within three months. The City Council has granted permission to the company to operate the motor for a period of sixty days, and before the expiration of that time application will be made, in the event of the invention proving successful, to make the permission perpetual. The public will await with much interest the result of the test, and if it proves as represented it promises to effect a complete revolution in the running of street cars in Baltimore, as other lines will doubtless substitute it as a motive power.

20 September 1876

174. Open cars served in the parks in summertime

175. Bus at Saint Paul Street campus of Goucher College

176. Electric cars first ran on Baltimore streets on 10 August 1885

177. Streetcars both plain and fancy transversed the city [c. 1880]

178. Horse-drawn streetcars replaced omnibuses, which had been operating since 1844

179. Streetcar repair yards

PICKPOCKETS ON CARS

ORGANIZED GANG IS AT WORK IN BALTIMORE.

Passenger Struggled With One Of Men On Madison-Avenue Car, But Without Success.

An organized gang of pickpockets, who, to use the police term, "tore things loose" in Philadelphia last week, are now believed to be operating in Baltimore, and the Police and Detective Departments are taking extraordinary measures to capture them.

Last evening the pickpockets are known to have worked on two different street cars, and secured a watch valued at $75, the property of Mr. Perry C. Orem of 1002 North Stricker street. The pickpockets attempted to rob Mr. Thomas Burns, a watchman and fireman at Druid Hill Park, while he was a passenger on a northbound Druid Hill-avenue car.

Mr. Orem's pocket was picked while he was on an Orleans-street line car, southbound. The manner in which the "dippers," as the police style this class of thieves, worked, proves conclusively, the detectives say, that the same men did the work.

Mr. Burns boarded the Druid Hill-avenue car at Fayette and Eutaw streets between 4.45 and 5 o'clock. The inside of the car was crowded, and a number of men were standing on the rear platform. There were two conductors on the car—one a "learner" and the other an experienced conductor. The latter was standing inside the car.

Just as Mr. Burns reached the platform he received a violent shove, and at the same moment felt something tug at his watch chain. He glanced down. His watch was hanging outside his vest pocket, and he saw a man's hand just unclosing from the timepiece. Seizing the man's hand, Mr. Burns exclaimed:

"Here's a pickpocket! He was just taking my watch when I caught him!"

The accusation created considerable excitement on the car. The alleged pickpocket struggled to get free, and Mr. Burns appealed to the conductor to assist in holding him. Much to Mr. Burns' disgust, the conductor refused to assist him, and the man, with a final effort, broke away and jumped from the car. Mr. Burns criticised the conductor for not helping him to hold the man until a policeman could be called. The conductor retaliated by threatening Mr. Burns with arrest if he did not cease berating him. The indignant passenger left the car at Eutaw street and Madison avenue and hurried to police headquarters, where he reported the affair and gave a detailed description of the man who had attempted to pick his pocket and also of the man who shoved him and who, he thought, was one of the gang.

Hardly had Mr. Burns finished making his report than Mr. Orem's complaint was received at detective headquarters. Mr. Orem was on the platform of a crowded car of the Orleans-street line. The conductor was collecting fares inside the car, and a man standing on the rear platform was attending to the bell cord and assisting in embarking and disembarking passengers. Mr. Orem did not realize that he had been relieved of his watch until the car was several blocks south of Baltimore street, although he remembers feeling a slight tug on the watch chain as a man back of him pushed against him. When he discovered that his pocket had been picked the self-constituted conductor and another man hastily alighted from the car. The description given by Mr. Burns of the two men who attempted to pick his pocket and the description given by Mr. Orem of the two men on the Orleans-street car tallies exactly.

Captain of Detectives Pumphrey appeared reluctant to admit that an organized gang of pickpockets was working in Baltimore, but when the reporter of The News mentioned the fact that two complaints had been made, the Captain said:

"We have information that the gang that worked Philadelphia last week is in this city, and that it was on the street cars last evening. In Philadelphia the thieves worked the same game, waiting until late in the evening to board the cars, when they were crowded. When the conductors are inside the cars collecting fares, one of the gang always offers to take charge of the bellcord and to assist passengers on and off the platform. While he is doing this, he jostles them, and his confederates do the "dipping and lifting."

3 February 1904

180. John Street car [c. 1885]

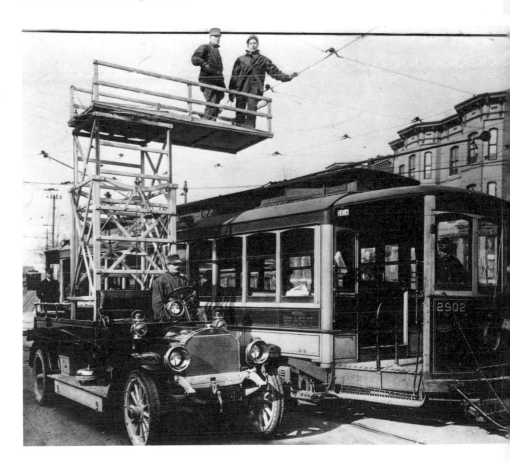

181. United Railways trouble wagon on North Avenue [1911]

182. Unidentified [1911]

In the fall of 1905 Miss Garrett, who was then living with Miss Thomas at Bryn Mawr, came to see Dr. Mary Sherwood and me to enlist our interest in the coming annual meeting of the National Women Suffrage Association to be held in Baltimore. She assumed we were suffragists. In the course of the conversation she turned to Dr. Sherwood and said: "Of course, Dr. Sherwood, you believe in suffrage." It was quite characteristic of the general attitude of many educated women that Dr. Sherwood responded: "Why, Miss Garrett, I haven't thought much on this subject, but I think I shall believe in it."

. . . The college of women of Baltimore, however, will recall with greater vividness the following Sunday afternoon when Miss Garrett invited them to come in for a cup of tea and a personal word from Miss Susan B. Anthony. . . . I never think of Miss Anthony as I saw her that afternoon, without recalling what Dr. Sherwood was wont to say when we had identified ourselves with the suffrage cause. She said it was good to be an American woman in this particular period of our country's history because we were the one class of human beings that was striving to obtain freedom and liberty, and that there was nothing in human experience so good for the soul as such a battle.

LILIAN WELSH, M.D., LL.D.
in *Reminiscences of Thirty Years in Baltimore*

LOVELY WOMAN NOW AND THEN

Lovely woman reads the GAZETTE extensively, and in the make-up of our paper it is our pleasant duty to cater to her taste, to give unto her such things as will edify; such things as will ennoble her loveliness; such things as will make her a better daughter, sister, wife, mother—a far better half of the great human family. We blush to confess that of late we have slighted her for politics, but she shall no more be slighted. Base purveyors to a base appetite, with ideas far beneath the level of lovely woman, vainly think to satisfy her longings with town talk, sewing-society gossip, choice bits of scandal and a column of deaths and marriages. But lovely woman has a soul above the effervescent, vanishing froth of these idly-sounding things. There are yearnings which a marriage will not satisfy, aching voids which gossips will not fill, heart-wounds which the demise of a well-to-do relative will scarcely heal. The woman of to-day has ideas. She has a mind, and she fain would have it strong. She reads Herbert Spencer, John Stuart Mill, Huxley, Tyndall, Darwin, mayhap the German philosophers, and probably—Tupper. The well-thumbed Longfellow, or Tennyson, or Bryant, or Browning, or even Swinburne, of other days; lies dust-grown on its half-forgotten shelf; centennial woman is deep in thought, and pegging away on the "true philosophy." She dreams of development and expansion, as applied to her sex. With dainty hand she draws aside the curtain of the future, and—behold the second centennial year!

It is the year of a presidential election. The great political giants are afield. From Baffin's Bay to the Isthmus of Panama the land rings with the shouts of the contending hosts. The Amazonian phalanx is armed and eager for the fray. Lovely woman in liberal numbers is busy at the hustings. She steps into her private balloon at Baltimore and away she speeds on the wings of the wind to San Francisco. Now and then she comes to an anchorage in the aerial sea, and from her suspended rostrum addresses monster meetings in the great cities from the Atlantic to the Pacific. The woman's national executive committee sits at Washington, and, by word of mouth, addresses mass meetings in all the states, for telegraphy is now a well-understood and much-used art. The day of election approaches. The administration having proved false to the people is in desperate straights. The committee on ways and means suggests bayonets at the polls, and quotes Grant in 1876 as a precedent. Throughout the land goes up the cry that the administration is in rebellion against the people. Woman joins the indignant throng and threatens to take up arms against oppression. But wiser counsels prevail. Cooler heads recount how, in 1876, the soldier-ridden states bore wrong with patience and looked to a liberty-loving land to lift them out of bondage. Statesmen, versed in the philosophy of events, urge patience and obedience, for the end, though long delayed, will come at last.

The day of election has come! Woman is at the polls, inside and out. She sitteth in the seat of judgment, she sitteth at the receipt of ballots; she passeth on the legality thereof. She standeth also about the polling booth, collareth the on-coming voter, and presseth ballots into his hands and into her hands. When the tale is told she shrieketh for victory or lamenteth over defeat; for though voting she is still woman. When the shades of night have fallen and streets are loud with huzzas of shouting men, lovely woman hies her to her home to "hush-a-by baby" and set things to rights. This is lovely woman of the future.

8 November 1876

183. Suffragist march [c. 1905]

Arrest of a Female Physician..

Mrs. Dr. Mary Walker was arrested yesterday on Front street, by Policeman Rose, because of having appeared on the street in male attire. She wore dark pants and a loose sack coat, reaching below the knees, and buttoned up to the chest, which was covered with lace and tied with ribbon, while on her head was a black straw flat. Her arrest caused considerable excitement. She was taken to the Middle District police station, when she inquired if the officer had any business to know her name. She was taken before Justice Hagerty, who dismissed her, and she left, declaring she would have redress.

23 July 1873

184. Harlem Park

99

185. Farewell [1917]

186. [1917]

187. Victory parade [after 11 November 1918]

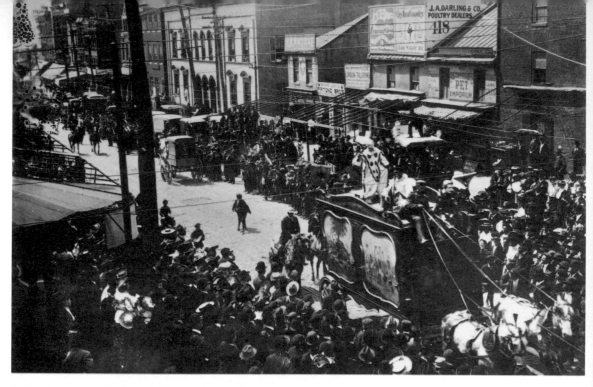

188. Opening of the German Beman Steamship Line [c. 1875]

189. Circus parade, North Eutaw Street [c. 1904–5]

190. Victory parade after World War I, Mount Royal Avenue

191. Watching a parade, Y.M.C.A. Building, Franklin Street

192. *Following pages:* Picnic at Gwynn Oak Park [c. 1900]

CITY STEAM BOTTLING HOUSE
CLUB GINGER ALE
WILD CHERRY SHERBET
ORANGE
CHAMPAGNE CIDERS
TONIC BEER
SODA WATER

193. Steamers along the wharves [1900–1903]

One hundred years ago when the first ship of the Old Bay Line, the *Georgia*, sailed down Chesapeake Bay, its patrons arrived in Baltimore by stage coach to embark for Norfolk, Virginia, where they took one of the dinky trains which served the Deep South. Today Baltimoreans take the boats of the Old Bay Line to Norfolk and Old Point Comfort as casually as they go to the movies, sometimes to spend their holidays at the beaches at the mouth of the bay, sometimes to break a long auto trip south by an overnight ride on one of the modern steamers which have replaced the early packets.

A few weeks ago we celebrated the one hundredth anniversary of the line with a trip down Chesapeake Bay on the *Warfield,* a birthday celebration in the grand manner, with Baltimore belles and gentlemen dressed as their ancestors had in the romantic days of its founding, and with waiters and porters in gaily colored short trousers and shirtwaists. From the top deck we watched the darkening skyline of Baltimore fade in the distance and were carried back in memory to the first trip on this oldest steamboat line in the United States and down the long years of its history.

We thought of Baltimore of 1826 when the citizens were aroused over the fact that public works of Pennsylvania and the Erie Canal had diverted a large portion of the trade which she needed. We thought of a city of 70,000 people two years later, when the Baltimore and Ohio Railroad was started, its harbor reaching into the busiest centers of the city and deep enough for the largest vessels afloat. When the Old Bay Line docks were built, the trains ran out onto the dock, the cowcatcher of the engine almost touching the gangplank of the boat.

During the War between the States—down South it is never called the Civil War—passengers on the Old Bay Line's boat saw the battle of the *Monitor* and the *Merrimac*. But in spite of the war, service was never entirely interrupted, even though one of its boats, the *William Selden,* was destroyed by the Confederates, and another, the *Adelaide,* was charted by the Union Navy for use as a transport and took part in the bombardments of Fort Hatteras and Fort Clark in 1861.

I was curious to know what the early boats of the Old Bay Line looked like and was told that after the War a period of great elegance was inaugurated. Deep-pile red carpets, gleaming brass spittoons, handrails, hardware and grapevine chandeliers furnished a gaudy background for the guests of the line in this flamboyant period. Heavy armchairs and ottomans were covered with crimson mohair plush, while the staterooms were provided with cherry bedsteads, carved panels and ornamental high head boards. The dressers had polished marble tops, and huge mirrors were everywhere. The Victorian influence reached its climax in the luxurious bridal suites which were the talk of the elite. The earliest boats were simpler affairs. The men were separated from the women, and if anyone wanted the steward in the middle of the night, he had to get up and find him.

Four times the records of the company have been destroyed—three times by fire and once by flood. But the Old Bay Line has survived its first century and is looking forward to the next hundred years of its life with undiminished vigor. And the captain still stands at the head of the gangplank to welcome each passenger aboard, a custom which has been unbroken since 1840.

RALPH PIERSON in *Travel,* July 1940

194. Light Street wharves [c. 1926]

195. Lurman family on an excursion to Wye Plantation, Eastern Shore

The Fifth Regiment—The Cape May Encampment.

The officers and members of the Fifth Regiment met on Saturday evening, in their armory, to make arrangements for the approaching excursion to Cape May on the 23d, where the command will go into camp for ten days. Colonel Jenkins and other officers of the regiment were present, and there was a conversational discussion of the subject, and much of the necessary preliminary arrangements were completed. It is expected that the number of muskets on parade at the sea shore will largely exceed that of the last encampment at Cape May, and the display promises to be the most attractive one ever made by the command. On Wednesday next the 200 tents necessary for the encampment will be taken to Cape May, and their erection superintended by Quartermaster Cromwell; and it is understood that a number of visitors from Baltimore will so time their annual excursion to the sea-shore as to be present when the regiment arrives, and remain there until the tents are "struck." The band will wear their new Austrian uniform, before described, and while in camp all members of the regiment will be allowed to wear as a fatigue dress suits of white flannel and straw hats trimmed with blue. The new instruments of the band, of silver, and costing $4,700, will also be brought into use for the first time. Several entertainments will be given the command, including a full dress ball at the Columbia House on the 25th instant, and the regiment will be reviewed by the Governors of Pennsylvania, New Jersey and Delaware, and also by his Excellency Governor Whyte, of Maryland, and Adjutant General Charles H. McBlair. The regiment will leave Baltimore on the night of the 23d instant, reach Cape May at 4.30 P. M. on the following day, and remain in camp ten days.

14 July 1873

196. Camp scene: Fifth Regiment, Maryland National Guard at Cape May, New Jersey [c. 1875]

Summertime in Baltimore was once synonymous with steamboat excursions. Every afternoon and evening from June to September throngs of men, women, and children escaped down the Bay to Annapolis, Bay Ridge, Tolchester, and beyond, in search of amusement and a breath of fresh air.

197. [c. 1880]

198. Patterson Park [c. 1880]

Parks provided a year-round respite from the hustle and bustle of the city. In 1827, William Patterson donated five acres for a "public walk," but the park that bears his name was not opened officially until 1853.

Riverview Park, which had been a beer garden since 1868, became an amusement park about 1900. In 1929 the land was purchased by Western Electric for its Point Breeze works.

Built in the 1890s, Electric Park was a favorite recreation spot. It was torn down in 1916.

199. Patterson Park

200. Royal Artillery Band performs at Riverview Park on the Patapsco River [after 1910]

201. Entrance to Patterson Park [1881]

202. Electric Park, on Belvedere Avenue near Reisterstown Road [c. 1900–10]

203. Music stand, Druid Hill Park [c. 1875]

204. Madison Avenue entrance to Druid Hill Park [after 1868]

The largest and most popular city park was Druid Hill (203–20). It was created out of 515 acres that the city purchased in 1860 from Lloyd Rogers for $513,000. By 1925 the park contained seventeen miles of roads, eight lakes, two reservoirs, two swimming pools, a zoo, and numerous pavilions.

205. Music pavilion

206. The photographer photographed

208. Grand Avenue leading to the mall and music pavilion

207. Council Grove Station and "dummy" engine [c. 1865–77]

209. Dedication of the Union Soldiers and Sailors Monument [6 November 1909]

Several large estates competed fiercely to be selected as *the* city park. Druid Hill was chosen because it included Mansion House, built in 1815 by Nicholas Rogers. The building was later converted into the zoo's bird house and business offices.

Most of the familiar structures around Druid Hill Park (203, 205, 207, 211) as well as the pagoda in Patterson Park, were designed by George A. Frederick, who also drew the plans for City Hall.

210. Mansion House [1880]

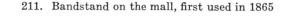

211. Bandstand on the mall, first used in 1865

212. Shepherd George McCleary with his flock, Mansion House [1906]

213. Druid Lake [1868]

214. Conservatory and tennis courts [after 1895]

215. Silver Lake

216. Bicycle boat

The Druid Hill Zoo was established by an act of the state legislature in 1876. It opened officially in 1881.

217. Bear pit, built 1880

218. Some days you hug the bear and some days the bear hugs you

219. Visiting the elk [after 1880]

An inventory made in 1880
showed that Druid Hill Zoo
contained 298 specimens:

215 deer
  1 three-legged duck
  3 swan
  2 black bears
  1 tiger cat
  2 prairie wolves
  1 gray fox
  1 nose bear
 13 monkeys
 15 white rats
  9 rabbits
  1 ostrich
  1 wild cat
  4 owls
  1 alligator
  2 small boa constrictors
 15 china geese

220. The camel house [1906]

FIRST DAY AT PIMLICO.

THREE FAVORITES CARRY THEIR COLORS TO VICTORY.

The Weather and Track All That Could Be Desired — Britannic, Tom Vaughn, Civil Service, Patrocles and Panama the Winners—Races on Other Tracks.

Seldom have the first events of the spring meeting at Pimlico been opened under more favorable auspices than yesterday. The weather was perfect, not too warm, and with a gentle breeze from the southwest that made the sport a rare pleasure. The attendance was not, however, up to the expectations of the management, and by the time the flag fell, shortly after three o'clock, for the first event on the program, only two thousand people had entered the grounds. It was a good-natured crowd, however, which thoroughly enjoyed the racing. Favorites were liberally backed, and the hungry ones managed to utilize the intermission between the events by eating ham sandwiches at twenty-five cents apiece, and talking horse with their neighbors on the poollawn. Adam Itzel's Fifth Regiment Band was in attendance. The musical program consisted of selections from "Il Palinte," "Les Huguenots," "Martha," "Little Tycoon," "Jack Sheppard" and the "College Overture." The famous old course certainly looked beautiful. The green grass, budding trees, and the prettily-constructed jumps added greatly to the picturesqueness of the place. The track is in a superb condition, and looked as well, if not better, than ever before.

221. The grandstand at Pimlico Race Track [c. 1888–1905]
222. The race [c. 1930]

8 May 1889

223. Horse show, Elkridge Kennel Club [1905]

224. Pimlico races [Autumn 1902]

Baltimore's Great Fire

Supplement to *Harper's Weekly*, February 13, 1904

An account from our special correspondent, giving some of the impressions of an eye-witness of one of the most disastrous fires our country has ever known

At ten o'clock Monday night, the entire business section of Baltimore, covering an area of about 140 acres, was a mass of ruins. Of the 2500 buildings which lay in the heart of Baltimore's business section little was left but huge masses of crumbling brick and stone and twisted girders. At that hour, as I saw from the roof of the highest business block left standing in Baltimore, just across the street from the point where the fire started, a fierce fire was raging in the warehouses and along the docks in the southeastern part of the city. Between these two points fires were blazing in the ruins, lighting up the skeleton walls and the piles of crumbling debris. These fires were allowed to burn; the real fighting at this hour was along the docks. Engines were stationed, however, at many points on the edge of the district bounded on the west by Liberty Street, on the north by Lexington Street, and on the east by Jones's Falls.

In many instances the firemen, worn out by more than thirty hours of work without sleep, played the streams of water upon threatened buildings by fastening the hose to dry goods boxes, while they themselves took shelter in doorways or went to sleep on the icy pavement. One of the firemen who had fallen asleep in the street was aroused by his captain, and when questioned by him as to how long he had been without sleep, replied: "A long time—three days. I don't remember." In one engine-house which I visited through the courtesy of Mr. Muth of Baltimore, a dozen men came in, some with slight injuries, which were cared for by the doctor who was present, others exhausted by their long fight with the fire. Just after the doctor left, an alarm sounded for a fire in another part of the city, and within three minutes these men who had been fighting the big fire since it began were on their way to protect the residential portion of the city.

The first engine to reach the scene of the fire in response to an automatic alarm in the warehouse of Hurst & Co., where the fire started, had only about two blocks to go to the scene of the fire. Captain Jordan of this company said to-night: "My first effort in order to get a line of hose into the burning building was to break open the door. I had hardly put my shoulder against it when I was warned by a cry from the men to run for my life, and at that instant there was a tremendous explosion, and the flames burst through the roof of the building and were carried immediately to the buildings adjoining." A high wind was blowing from the southwest, and the fire spread rapidly toward the northeast, in the direction of the Court House, Post Office, and City Hall, consuming, one after another, great mercantile houses in its path. When the fire had reached Lexington Street, at the junction of North Calvert Street, the wind suddenly veered in the opposite direction. It was this fortunate circumstance which saved not only the city buildings, the Post Office, Court House, and City Hall, but prevented the spread of the fire to the home district north of Lexington Street. As it was, the fire swept back to St. Paul Street and down and across the parallel and intersecting streets toward the southeastern part of the city, until for a distance of more than ten blocks the magnificent buildings in the financial district of the city had either been gutted by the flames or dynamited in hope of preventing the spread of the flames. Some idea of the rapidity with which the fire spread through many of the so-called "fire-proof" buildings may be had from the fact that while the first automatic alarm was received at 10:48, the clock in the Maryland Trust Company, at the northwest corner of Calvert and German streets, four blocks from the point where the fire started, was stopped by the flames at twenty minutes past eleven. This building was one of the few whose walls were left standing, although the interior was thoroughly destroyed as if it had been of paper. I was told, however, that here, as in many of the trust buildings, the contents of the vaults were not seriously injured. One trust company was out of the fire district. Within two doors of the *Sun* office, which is now in ruins, two watchmen were locked in a trust building during the fire. One of the watchmen was confined in a vault, and could only be released with the time lock. While all the other buildings in this neighborhood were destroyed, this one building happened to escape serious injury.

It was the general impression on Monday afternoon that martial law had already been established. Federal troops and militia were patrolling all the streets bordering on the fire district, and

227. 1 A.M. 8 February: Shot Tower, *center;* City Hall, *right.* The glow of the fire could be seen clearly one hundred miles away

no one was allowed to pass without a permit from the Attorney-General or from the president of the Police Commissioners. As a matter of fact, the troops were in control of the city, but it required a special session of the Legislature to authorize the Governor to declare martial law. The same General Assembly at Annapolis passed a bill authorizing Governor Warfield to declare ten successive legal holidays, in order to protect the financial interests of the city by extending credit.

Outside the firelines tens of thousands of people, held in check by the drawn bayonets of the militia, stood all day and late into the night gazing over the ruins. Within the lines, even as late as Monday afternoon and evening, one had not to go very far in any direction before being stopped by piles of smouldering debris, or by blinding, suffocating smoke from the cellars and interiors of those buildings of which a part of the walls still remained standing.

A tangled network of electric wires was held suspended over the streets of the ruined district, sometimes reaching from half the height of a tottering wall to the ground.

Of the Baltimore *Sun* building, the first iron building to be built in America, only four pillars were left standing. Just around the corner, the Merchants Club, and next door to that the Stock Exchange Building were completely ruined. Farther on, at the head of German Street, I saw through a grating a fierce blaze from the coal bins in the cellar of the First National Bank. Of this bank there was nothing left but the walls.

The fire covered an area which in New York might be included in the district from Wall Street to Park Row and from Broadway east to the river-front; it is a conservative estimate to place the loss at one hundred million dollars.

226. Hose Company No. 15 at the Manufacturers' Bank

TEN THOUSAND AT STATION.

Washington's Firemen Given an Ovation on Their Arrival.

H. P. Baldwin, traveling passenger agent of the Baltimore and Ohio, was on the train which carried Chief Belt and the first two companies to Baltimore. He returned last night. To a Post reporter he said:

"When we were at Relay, nine miles from Baltimore, we saw the black smoke and flames leaping into the air far above the city. Ten thousand people were at Camden station, Baltimore, when we arrived. Every preparation had been made to unload the fire apparatus. As the two companies dashed down the street, cheers from men and women for an instant challenged in volume the noise the fire was making. Washington was the first to send aid. Philadelphia sent help before Wilmington."

The water plugs of the Washington engines were too small for the hydrants, and Chief Belt was forced to run the hose down into the sewer.

Mr. Baldwin said the streams of water thrown on buildings seemed to act more like oil than water.

"Big, stalwart men were standing on the street weeping," said Mr. Baldwin. "I saw many men in tears embrace one another in their common sorrow. Women were caught in the dense crowd and carried away fainting."

8 February 1904

228. Hoses and ladders on an unidentified street

229. Lombard and Liberty streets

230. *Following pages:* View from the Shot Tower of the entire fire district, from Jones Falls *at left,* to City Hall, *right*

231. Ruins of the Continental Trust Building

232. Engine No. 15, deserted after the collapse of the Hurst Building, where the fire started

233. Hopkins Savings Bank

234. The fire district

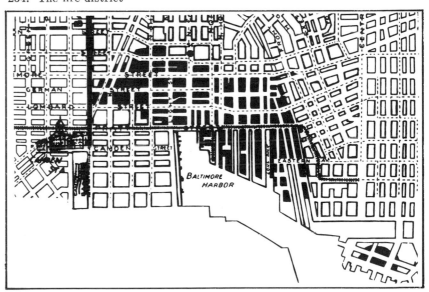

235. Ruins of the Maryland Institute (*see* 69)

236. Ruins of an unidentified street

237. H. C. Kirk, Jr., *right*, inspecting damage suffered by Samuel Kirk and Sons

238. The Bendann brothers inspect the ruins of their premises at 105 East Baltimore Street

WALKING AMONG THE RUINS

Those Who Get Within Fire Lines Find Little To Cheer Them.

By 10:30 o'clock to-day several squares of Baltimore street, which had been devastated, and the walls crumbled, had cooled sufficiently to enable pedestrians to walk between the ruins. Many business men whose places of business were in this district strolled arm in arm down the street as far as they dared. In many cases they were unable to locate where their business houses stood. Later the danger of being struck by falling walls became so great that a cordon of militia was placed around the western end of the burned district, and refused to allow any one, whether the possessor of a badge or pass or not, to go through the lines.

9 February 1904

239. *Opposite:* The Post Office and City H

240. A view of the flattened city blocks, from Federal Hill

THE SUN AND THE FIRE

In the Baltimore fire of February 7-8, 1904, which laid waste the business section of the city and destroyed The Sun building and all the other newspaper offices except one. The Sun with characteristic enterprise, did not omit a single issue, but kept on regularly every day without a break, serving its subscribers by mail and carriers, and its advertisers, who, in that emergency needed its services more than ever before.

Realizing the possibility that the disaster would involve the Sun building at the S. E. corner of Baltimore and South streets, preparations were begun early in the forenoon of Sunday to seek a place for the safe storage of the valuable files of the paper in bound volumes from May 17, 1837 to date; of the mailing lists of subscribers; of the books of the counting-room and such other appurtenances as could be saved.

The moving began at 4 P. M., and was hastened by the nearer and nearer approach of the flames, until shortly after midnight when the building was enveloped in flames. Some of the effects saved in the later hours of the night, were charred.

The directing manager of the paper and business manager took personal supervision of all the details necessary for continued publication, and saving valuable effects. In good time, before the wires were burned, negotiations were made with *The Washington Evening Star* for printing the Monday morning edition and for temporary service until the effects of the disaster could be mastered fully. A special train of the Baltimore & Ohio Railroad was engaged to wait for transferring at a moment's notice a sufficient force of the staff of The Sun from one city to the other, to finish the work of getting out the edition. At the same time everything was kept in readiness, with steam up and lights burning to go ahead in Baltimore if The Sun building should escape.

By eleven o'clock, however, all hope was abandoned, and the order was given to proceed to Washington. A detail from the editorial staff, and the forces of the composing room, of the mailing department, the stereotypers and several clerks of the counting-room were transferred from Baltimore to Washington in 45 minutes by the B. & O. railroad. Regular work on the edition did not cease in Baltimore until the very moment of departure. There was no excitement or hurry. Everybody knew his place, and the direction was cool and methodical.

In Washington City *The Evening Star* office was found ready in all its departments, with lights burning, steam up, and telegraph wires ready for use. The staff of The Sun went to work in the different departments, just as if they were at home in their own quarters. The Monday morning edition was printed on *The Evening Star* presses and distributed on regular time. A special train of the B. & O. brought the papers to Camden Station where the Baltimore City carriers received them and distributed them over their routes. The mail edition was dispatched from the postoffice in Washington City, so that all subscribers were supplied on Monday morning while The Sun office was a heap of scrap iron and the conflagration was not yet under control. It was the first and only Baltimore paper to get out an early edition that day. A still later edition supplied further details of the fire and other news.

While operations were going on in Washington, the home contingent of the editorial and reporting staff, and the clerical force of the counting-room, took possession of The Sun Job Printing House, at the S. W. corner of Calvert and Saratoga streets, which was a veritable house of refuge in an emergency. Here the details of the fire and other local news were collected and forwarded by wire or by special messenger every hour of the day to the section of the staff operating in Washington. Here, too, the needs of the crippled business interests of Baltimore were promptly and uninterruptedly attended to.

By degrees the necessary machinery was secured and installed in the temporary quarters at Calvert and Saratoga streets. Two quadruple presses, rescued from the vaults of the Sun Iron building in damaged condition, were repaired and put to work. All the linotype machines, stereotype equipment, engines, boilers, dynamos, etc., were destroyed in the old establishment, together with one of the latest Hoe Quadruple Presses, the parts of which were melted in the heat, or crushed into scrap steel by the falling in of the superstructure upon it.

The work devolving upon the A. S. Abell Co. was practically that of creating a new plant on the costly lines of modern newspaper printing office equipment, in the temporary quarters, which had been fortunately provided as an emergency building by the foresight of the late president of the company, Mr. Edwin F. Abell, whose death occurred February 28.

All facilities for doing business at Saratoga and Calvert streets were fully completed in two months, when on April 7, the whole Sun force was reunited in the temporary home in Baltimore.

On the close of the period of The Sun's tenancy *The Evening Star* of April 7, gave warm expression to the feeling of kindness which marked the relations of the two organizations throughout, and said: "*The Evening Star* could not wish for more agreeable or welcome guests, for more considerate transient occupants of its establishment, for more thoughtful or careful employes of all grades and classes. If *The Evening Star* was in a position by reason of its mechanical equipment to render The Sun this service, The Sun, on its part, was in a position to make the best and most thoughtful use of every facility placed at its disposal."

In announcing its home-coming The Sun of April 7, said: "It felt under every obligation of friendship and gratitude to put on record publicly its appreciation of the sacrifices made by *The Washington Evening Star* in its willingness to go to the limit of its resources to help a newspaper friend in the day of adversity. *The Evening Star* has given the journalistic world an exhibition of practical friendship and good-fellowship which is almost without parallel."

The publishers of The Sun also expressed "their deep appreciation of the loyal services of its own corps and staff in every department, who in an hour of need so earnestly and intelligently mastered the difficulties which none but newspaper men can properly estimate and which to those not newspaper men would have seemed insurmountable obstacles. To The Sun's employes, however, there is no such word as fail, and to this is due the fact that The Sun was the only newspaper in the city which published its regular editions Monday, February 8, delivering by mail and carrier almost on the same schedule time as if no catastrophe had occurred."

1905 Sunpapers Almanac

241. Damage to the wharves

242. Rebuilding Saint Paul Street

LADIES IN NEW FIELD

Have Opened "Lunch Rooms" In Various Parts Of Town.

Will Relinquish Social Duties To Serve Midday Repast To Business Men—Some Features.

While the fire was the cause of temporarily suspending some enterprises, it has been rseponsible for the formation of others, and this is noticeable in the number of lunch-rooms that have started up recently. In fact, the lunch-room business is enjoying a great boom, and the field has been entered by a number of ladies identified with the social life of Baltimore.

Realizing the possibilities in the lunch-room line, several prominent women have rented quarters in the section of the city where corporations and commercial houses have transferred their forces. Many of those who conducted such establishments in the district that was burned have not reopened, and the patronage of midday lunchers will be sought by a class of caterers to the public palate that has not heretofore conducted such places. The ladies embarking in the new enterprise expect to have men for customers in the majority of cases, and prefer the masculine "lunch-room" to the effeminate "tea-room."

Mrs. Edward T. Norris and Miss Fannie Gray have opened their place in the basement of the old Maryland Club Building, corner of Franklin and Cathedral streets. The entrance is in the rear, on Hamilton street.

Mrs. Laura Turnbull, proprietor of the Bristol, on Eutaw place, has opened the Virginia Lunchroom, at 12 East Pleasant street, near Charles street, and back of the Woman's Industrial Exchange. A number of lawyers, real estate agents, insurance men and others have taken offices in that part of the town, and the Woman's Industrial Exchange has been unable to accommodate all the hungry people. Mrs. Turnbull expects to get the overflow, as well as an individual line of patrons. As the name of her establishment indicates, Mrs. Turnbull, who is from Petersburg and a daughter of Judge Hicks of Virginia, will endeavor to serve edibles famous in the Old Dominion, such as old ham sandwiches, waffles and corn bread. The Maryland ladies will offer delicacies typical of their State also, and Maryland biscuit will be included in the menu.

Miss Rebecca Bolling and Miss Ethel Woods, both young girls in society, have formed a partnership to conduct a lunchroom at the corner of Pratt and Greene streets. One of the branches of the Baltimore and Ohio Railroad is located there, and many business men have offices in the neighborhood.

All of the ladies will give their personal attention to running their respective enterprises, and are notifying their male friends that they will expect their patronage. The innovation in the lunch-room business is the talk of the uptown clubs; and, metaphorically speaking, the men take their hats off to the promoters and admire their grit and pluck.

20 February 1904

134

243. Saint Paul Street

TRAINS ON SCHEDULE TIME

No Extras Put On By Railroads Entering City, However.

No extra trains are being put on any of the railroads entering Baltimore. An official of one of the roads said this morning that no extra trains would be put in service, and thath there was a tacit understanding to that effect between the managers of the operating departments, the intention being to thus aid in keeping down the crowds and avoiding possible looting in the crush. To-day all trains are running on schedule time and carrying hundreds both ways, many leaving the city to visit friends elsewhere pending a settling of conditions and many more making the change for the purpose of securing employment in other cities.

In spite of the fact that no extra trains are run and that the railroad people assert they are not putting an extra coach on any train, the report has been broadcast that excursion trains have been run. This report arose, doubtless, from the the tremendous crowds at all stations, which have increased exceedingly since the first rush for the city began. All day Sunday the trains showed increase of traffic. Yesterday not a train reached Baltimore which was not packed to the point of suffocation, and the late trains yesterday, especially from Washington, Philadelphia, New York, and points east, were crowded to the guards. A News employe came from the upper part of New York State on the Pennsylvania Railroad train, leaving New York at 1 o'clock yesterday afternoon. In New York interest in the disaster was intense, and on the train there was no other topic of conversation. When the train left Hoboken there was not a seat in any car, excepting the Pullmans, and by the time Wilmington was reached people were standing in the day coaches as thickly as they would be found in a Baltimore street car during the rush hour. All the way down there were eager knots of people discussing every new feature of the news. One woman in the back of a Pullman became hysterical.

9 February 1904

244. Baltimore and Holliday streets

245. Tearing down an unsafe wall

246. West from Saint Paul and Baltimore streets [1904]

Thinks That City Should Have Underground Cars.

To the Editor of The News:

I have for years wondered why a plan for a subway for Baltimore was not discussed. Baltimore street has been getting worse and worse, so that it is difficult to cross, and it is no unusual thing to see cars blocks the street for three or four blocks or more. With a subway, the cars would disappear, of course; wires, poles, and other objectionable and unsightly things would depart. Boston had no greater need of her subway when it was built than we have now, and, besides, no matter what is done with streets by way of widening, etc., Baltimore street will still be the main thoroughfare. The subway should be built as New York City is building hers—by the city, at no cost, as rentals more than pay for interest on bonds, etc. I hope we will have wider streets, etc., and many other of the good things mentioned in your paper (provided they can be arranged for speedily); but it seems to me a subway under Baltimore street is more important to the Baltimore that is to be than any of them.

LOUIS CASSARD, JR.

19 February 1904

247. West from Saint Paul and Baltimore streets [1906]

248. *Following pages:* Baltimore skyline from Federal Hill, two years after the fire [1906]

The New City of Baltimore

John Wilber Jenkins, in *The World's Work*, 1914

The visitor to the Star Spangled Banner Centennial, which celebrated the repulse of the British at Fort McHenry and North Point and the writing of the national anthem by Francis Scott Key, found that out of the old Baltimore has grown a new city—new in spirit as well as in its buildings, streets, parks, sewers, and docks.

It was the great fire of February 7 and 8, 1904 that stirred up the ancient town. For a generation the town had been going along in its slow and steady way, growing surely but gradually, but in many important respects it was far behind cities not half its size. When the flames died down Monday night, after blazing fiercely since Sunday morning, the citizens saw the heart of the business district in ruins, 2,200 buildings in ashes, and more than $100,000,000 worth of property destroyed. But Baltimore declined the help from New York and a dozen other financial centres so generously offered and began the work of rebuilding with its own resources.

And it was a stupendous task that Baltimore began ten years ago. A Burnt District Commission was created and began to lay out new street lines downtown in the place of the old streets which were narrow and badly congested. Light Street, which runs from Baltimore Street along the wharves where Chesapeake Bay steamers land, was transformed from a narrow 45-foot bed to a broad thoroughfare 125 feet wide. Pratt Street was widened from 66 feet to 120 feet, relieving the congestion caused by the thousands of teams and cars that handle the traffic to wharves from which steamers sail for Boston, Savannah, Jacksonville, and the West Indies. What had been a mere gorge in front of the classic Court House was broadened into a plaza. South Charles Street, Hanover, Hopkins Place, Calvert, Commerce, and Lombard streets and West Falls Avenue were all widened. Old Marsh Market Place was turned into a large plaza and immense wholesale and retail markets for the handling of oysters, fish, fruit, and produce were built, stretching in a long line almost from Baltimore Street to the waterfront. On the new and wider streets grew new and better buildings. The fire that seemed the most terrible of calamities proved a blessing in disguise, for it forced the creation of an entirely new district, and the downtown section of Baltimore has to-day more new buildings than are in a similar area in any other city in the United States except San Francisco.

But it did more than that. It compelled merchants in other sections to modernize their stores and warehouses to keep pace with those in the "Burnt District," and this has resulted in improvement all over the city. With its new business centre, Baltimore became ashamed of its open sewers and cobblestone pavements, of its old docks and wharves and narrow streets, and while it was rebuilding its business district it set about to make other large improvements.

The long stretch of docks and wharves were owned by railroad or steamship corporations which had the power to levy toll on commerce or shut out new steamship lines. The city decided to spend $6,000,000 in acquiring sections of the waterfront and beginning a system of municipally owned piers. The big recreation pier at the foot of Broadway, just completed and opened last July, combines facilities for steamers and smaller boats with immense floors for dancing and playgrounds, all free to the public. It is in the midst of a congested district, and sometimes as many as 20,000 persons take advantage of it in a single day and night. The latest report of the United States Army Engineers to Congress shows that Baltimore now has 152 docks and wharves, 18 miles of available waterfront in the city and an almost unlimited amount farther down toward the Bay, has 34 regular steamship lines and 1,300 craft engaged in the coastwise and Chesapeake Bay trade.

250. The Bromo Seltzer Building, Eutaw and Lombard streets. Height of tower, with bottle, was 357 feet. The bottle was 10,000,000 times larger than the ten-cent original, weighed seventeen tons, and contained 596 electric lights

There was no street worth the name running parallel with the long line of docks from Light Street to Locust Point, where the steamers from Europe land their passengers and cargoes. So the city has cut a street 160 feet wide from Light Street to Locust Point, curving along this stretch of harbor, and has named it "Key Highway," for it will eventually be extended to Fort McHenry, from which floated the star-spangled banner that inspired Francis Scott Key to write his immortal song. The War Department has just turned Fort McHenry over to the city for preservation and use as a public park, and at the edge of the Fort work is beginning on the new Immigration Station that will cost $550,000 and provide for the thousands of immigrants that land here.

Baltimore was a century behind modern cities in sanitation. Though the better class residences and business houses were provided for by privately owned systems, there were 70,000 earth closets and hundreds of miles of open sewers menacing health. Typhoid fever destroyed its hundreds. After the fire, the long-postponed resolve to build a real sewerage system was put into effect. A loan of $10,000,000 was voted and a commission created, which selected Mr. Calvin W. Hendrick as chief engineer, and within two years after the fire active work was begun. As Mr. Hendrick told a convention of engineers the task was to "do a hundred years of work in seven years."

Seven hundred miles of pipes had to be laid under buildings and streets. At times the rate of construction has been 140 miles a year. The first loan of $10,000,000 was not sufficient to bring it half way toward completion. Another loan of $10,000,000 followed; then $3,000,000 more to provide for the new residential sections. The complete system for the city and suburbs will probably cost as much as $30,000,000. But it has been built to accommodate a million residents. The immense outfall sewer, five and one half miles long, is so large that on their tour of inspection the governor, mayor, and party rode through it in automobiles, the 20-foot breadth, 12 feet at the base, giving plenty of room for the motor-cars. The disposal plant at Back River covers forty acres.

At the time of the fire Baltimore had more cobblestones and rough pavement than any other American city. Chairman R. Keith Compton, of the Paving Commission, found 5,000,000 square yards of cobblestones, "enough," as he remarked, "to make an 18-foot road nearly five hundred miles long." There were many miles of Belgian blocks and nondescript rough stone pavements,

251.   Light Street wharves, Conway Street, *left* [1912].

252. Electric wire being laid under Howard Street [1901]

253. Sewer inspection [before 1914]

and streets that were hardly paved at all. So when the sewerage system was well underway, Baltimore started work on "the biggest paving job on earth." The city is now laying smooth paving at the rate of ten miles a month, and the pavers are at work on twenty streets at the same time. In the business section, where street cars and trucks crowd in an almost continuous line, the paving has been done by the block without interrupting traffic. Asphalt is used, for the most part, though stone is necessary on heavy teeming streets. In the suburbs, miles of bitulithic pavement have been laid. The cost runs far into the millions, but the people pay the bill gladly, as they can see the results at every step. The county and suburbs have followed the city's example, and even such ancient thoroughfares as the old York Road have had their mudholes replaced with a surface as smooth as a floor. And the state is constructing an extensive system that will soon place Maryland near the top among the "good roads" states.

One of the most remarkable pieces of engineering accomplished in recent years has been the transformation of Jones Falls, which had degenerated into an open sewer, running from the north clear through the city down to the waterfront, into a splendid concrete street. That stream, with its frequent floods, had caused so much damage that a generation ago $2,000,000 was spent confining it with stone retaining walls, which still did not prevent occasional overflows.

The "Falls" was an offense to eyes and nostrils and a constant menace. Engineer Hendrick found it one of the most trying problems he had to deal with. He devised a plan to force the stream into a huge concrete pipe, lay another pipe as a storm-water sewer, and others to care for ordinary sewage. Over this has been laid a concrete bed which is covered with paving. Thus the stream has been converted into a modern highway, giving a new boulevard from Union Station down to Baltimore Street, the "Fallsway." To lift the street from Jones Falls Valley to the level of Mount Royal Avenue it was necessary to construct a huge viaduct which gives an easy ascent. The drainage tunnel, seventy-one feet below the surface of Guilford Avenue, is so large that on June 4th, the entire American Society of Civil Engineers was entertained at a banquet in the 29-foot tube. The last section of the Fallsway is just being completed. The entire cost of the improvements is not much more than the $2,000,000 that was spent on the old retaining walls.

At the time the fire occurred, Mr. Frederick Law Olmsted and his staff had just completed the survey and report which they

254. Union Station and Jones Falls [c. 1910]

256. Charles Street Boulevard at entrance to the Homewood campus of The Johns Hopkins University [c. 1910]

made to the Municipal Art Society and in which they outlined a plan to develop a vast park system, linking the existing parks by boulevards, and to acquire the most beautiful tracts and streams in the suburbs. Away back in 1859, when the first horse-car lines were started, astute aldermen required them to contribute 20 per cent of their receipts to maintain the parks, then just being created. This percentage was found too high, but it was not reduced until 1874, when it was placed at 12 per cent. When the various electric lines were merged into the United Railways, which owns all city and suburban lines, the tax was fixed for the older lines at 9 per cent, and for the less profitable suburban lines as low as 2 to 3 per cent. This tax yields a constantly increasing revenue, which can be applied only to parks and boulevards.

Mayor Richard M. Venable, president of the Park Board, a leading lawyer, a man of vision, began at once to put the Olmsted plan into effect. Gwynns Falls, which presents a wonderful combination of high hills and limpid water, had been acquired and was converted into five miles of as beautiful a natural park as

any city possesses. Wyman Park, on Charles Street, just in front of the new Johns Hopkins campus, and numerous other beauty spots were included in the system. Charles Street in that section was converted into the Parkway, a broad boulevard with double drives. All around and beyond it is growing up one of the finest residential sections in the country.

On the hills beyond Wyman Park are rising the new buildings of Johns Hopkins University. From the Hopkins University and Wyman Park a boulevard stretches to the east, running through the new Venable Park to Montebello. There will be a driveway to Clifton Park; and, a few blocks below, the boulevard Broadway gives an attractive drive to the large Patterson Park in the southern section. To the west the boulevard runs to Druid Hill Park and from that point will be carried through the Mount Alto and Forest Park section to Gwynns Falls Park, which runs far into the southwest. So this dream of Venable and Olmsted of a chain of parks and boulevards around the entire city is becoming a reality. And it has cost the taxpayers hardly anything, being paid for by the tax on the street car system that benefits from it.

255. Howard Street [c. 1914]

257. Locker room at School No. 108 on Caroline Street [11 July 1922]

258. Swimming pool at Gwynns Falls

When Rev. Dr. Thomas M. Beadenkoff in 1893 erected his first little "shack" with a fund of only $500 back of it, he little dreamed that it would develop into an extensive system of public baths. Baltimore now has five indoor cleansing baths, with 200 cabins, which accommodate 500,000 persons a year; five large swimming pools in parks and on the river front to which many thousands resort in summer; and a system of portable baths which originated here, small houses which are carried from one street corner to another in the crowded sections and afford hot and cold shower baths for 75,000 persons every year. With the recent addition of four acres, the pool in Patterson Park is probably the largest enclosed swimming pool in the world. Mr. Henry Walters has erected and endowed a series of public baths. In addition there are a number of "wash houses," where women who have no servants bring their laundry and wash their clothes.

With all its improvements Baltimore has maintained perhaps its chief, if its least spectacular, virtue. It is still essentially a city of homes, for those who dwell in apartments form a very small percentage of the population, and tenements are few. There are hundreds of blocks of little one-family houses in Baltimore. These "two-story houses," as they are called, though they make many streets long stretches of monotony, provide decent and comfortable homes for wage earners. For $15 or $20 a month a man can have his own house, of six or eight rooms, with bath, and often with stationary wash tubs, cemented cellars, and conveniences that in other cities the poor cannot hope for. He can buy that house on partial payments by adding $5 a month to his rent money. In some sections, like Highlandtown and Canton, rents are as low as $10 a month. He can take his basket and go to Lexington or one of the other big markets and get his meats, vegetables, fruits, and entire food supply for less than in almost any other city, for here at the head of the Chesapeake is the heart of the trucking and canning section. All kinds of vegetables, fruits, oysters, fish, and crabs are abundant, and the menu is varied. These two-story houses are built steadily at the rate of two thousand a year, and perhaps half as many more go up in the outlying districts. Tenements cannot compete with them—in price plus desirability.

Many people went to Baltimore to celebrate the one hundredth anniversary of the writing of the national song; the glory of this they all felt. What they saw was the remarkable work that marks the tenth anniversary of the great fire that awakened Baltimore.

259. Lexington Street and Park Avenue [c. 1920s]

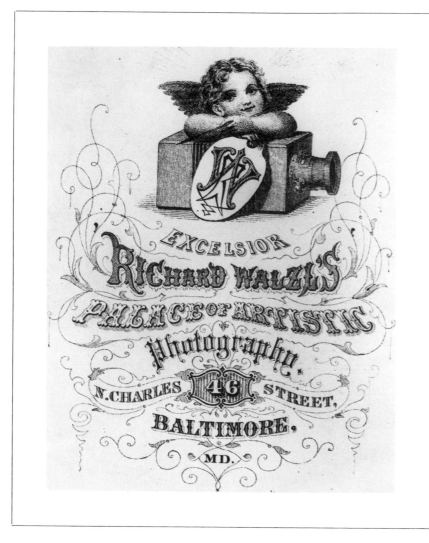

Designed by Mame Warren, Marion E. Warren
and Gerard A. Valerio

Edited by Mary Veronica Amoss and Jane Warth

This book was composed in Linotype Century and
Bauer Bodoni by the Service Composition
Company, Baltimore, Maryland.

It was printed on 80-lb. Warren's Lustro Offset
Enamel paper by the Collins Lithographing and
Printing Company, Baltimore, Maryland, and
bound in Holliston cloth by the Optic Bindery,
Baltimore, Maryland.

SOURCES FOR PHOTOGRAPHS

Baltimore Gas and Electric Company: 252; Baltimore and Ohio Railroad, *The Book of the Royal Blue*: 234; Enoch Pratt Free Library: 11, 17, 21, 26, 27, 28, 29, 30, 37, 43, 89, 95, 108, 109, 132, 143, 192, 209, 213, 216, 225, 227, 228, 229, 235, 237; Elouise Harding: 62, 93, 98, 134, 193, 200, 221, 241, 250, 254, 259; Allan Hirsh, Jr.: 55, 80, 125, 142, 214, 222, 256; Ross Kelbaugh: 8, 39, 65, 69, 71, 75, 76, 94, 102, 110, 156, 157, 207; Library of Congress: 7, 9, 40, 47, 48, 50, 74, 103, 106, 107, 127, 129, 130, 131, 212, 220, 231, 233, 245; Michael Luby: 144; Maryland Historical Society: 1, 2, 5, 6, 12, 18, 19, 20, 22, 23, 24, 31, 32, 33, 34, 35, 36, 38, 41, 44, 45, 46, 49, 51, 52, 53, 56, 57, 58, 59, 60, 61, 63, 64, 66, 67, 68, 70, 72, 73, 77, 78, 79, 86, 91, 92, 96, 97, 101, 111, 115, 116, 118, 119, 120, 121, 122, 123, 124, 126, 128, 133, 135, 136, 137, 138, 139, 140, 141, 145, 146, 147, 148, 149, 150, 153, 154, 155, 158, 159, 160, 161, 162, 163, 164, 165, 166, 167, 169, 170, 171, 172, 173, 174, 175, 176, 177, 178, 179, 180, 181, 182, 183, 184, 187, 188, 189, 190, 194, 195, 196, 197, 198, 201, 203, 206, 210, 211, 215, 217, 218, 219, 223, 224, 226, 230, 236, 238, 239, 240, 242, 243, 244, 246, 247, 248, 249, 253; James Mason: front endsheet; Talbot County Historical Society: 251; Edward L. Bafford Photography Collection, University of Maryland Baltimore County: 54, 151, 152, 185, 186, 191, 255, 257, 258, back endsheet; Norman Vach: 16, 42; M. E. Warren: 10, 202; Beverly and Jack Wilgus: 13, 14, 15, 25, 81, 82, 83, 84, 85, 87, 88, 90, 99, 100, 104, 105, 112, 114, 117, 168, 199, 204, 205, 208, 232; G. Zlotowitz: 113

PHOTOGRAPHERS

W. M. Ashman: 63, 148; David Bachrach (& Company): 16, 32, 42, 69, 149, 196, 213; Bendann: 124; Benet (family album): 116, 137, 141; Henry H. Clark: 33; Culver: 95; Hughes Company: 2, 22, 54, 77, 79, 119, 120, 121, 140, 142, 151, 152, 154, 170, 185, 186, 191, 248, 255, 257, 258, back endsheet; Jeffries: 175; F. W. Muller: 230, 239; William A. Raw: 232; D. C. Redington: 161; Henry Rinn, Jr.: 62, 93, 98, 134, 167, 193, 200, 219, 221, 241, 250, 254, 259; J. H. Schaefer: 96, 251; J. W. Schaefer: 240; George W. Schilling: 238; William Shorey: 12; Richard Walzl: 90; William H. Weaver: 5, 41, 46, 82, 83, 99, 168; G. E. Wood: 81; Thomas Worthington (*Sunpapers*): 11

PUBLISHERS

E. & H. T. Anthony: 14, 39; Bell & Brothers: 40; W. M. Chase: 13, 15, 34, 44, 71, 74, 75, 76, 88, 100, 102, 112, 114, 117, 118, 188, 198, 201, 204, 208, 215; Detroit Publishing Company: 7, 48, 50, 103, 107, 127, 129, 130, 131, 212, 220; Keystone View Company: 105, 106; J. W. & J. S. Moulton: 25; Ottenheimer Publishing Company: 55, 80, 125, 222, 256; Stewart & Doyle: 180; D. R. Stiltz & Company: 68, 126; Underwood & Underwood: 47; Van Wagner & Dyer: 178

Note: Numbers refer to photographic plates.